Westla

CW01370489

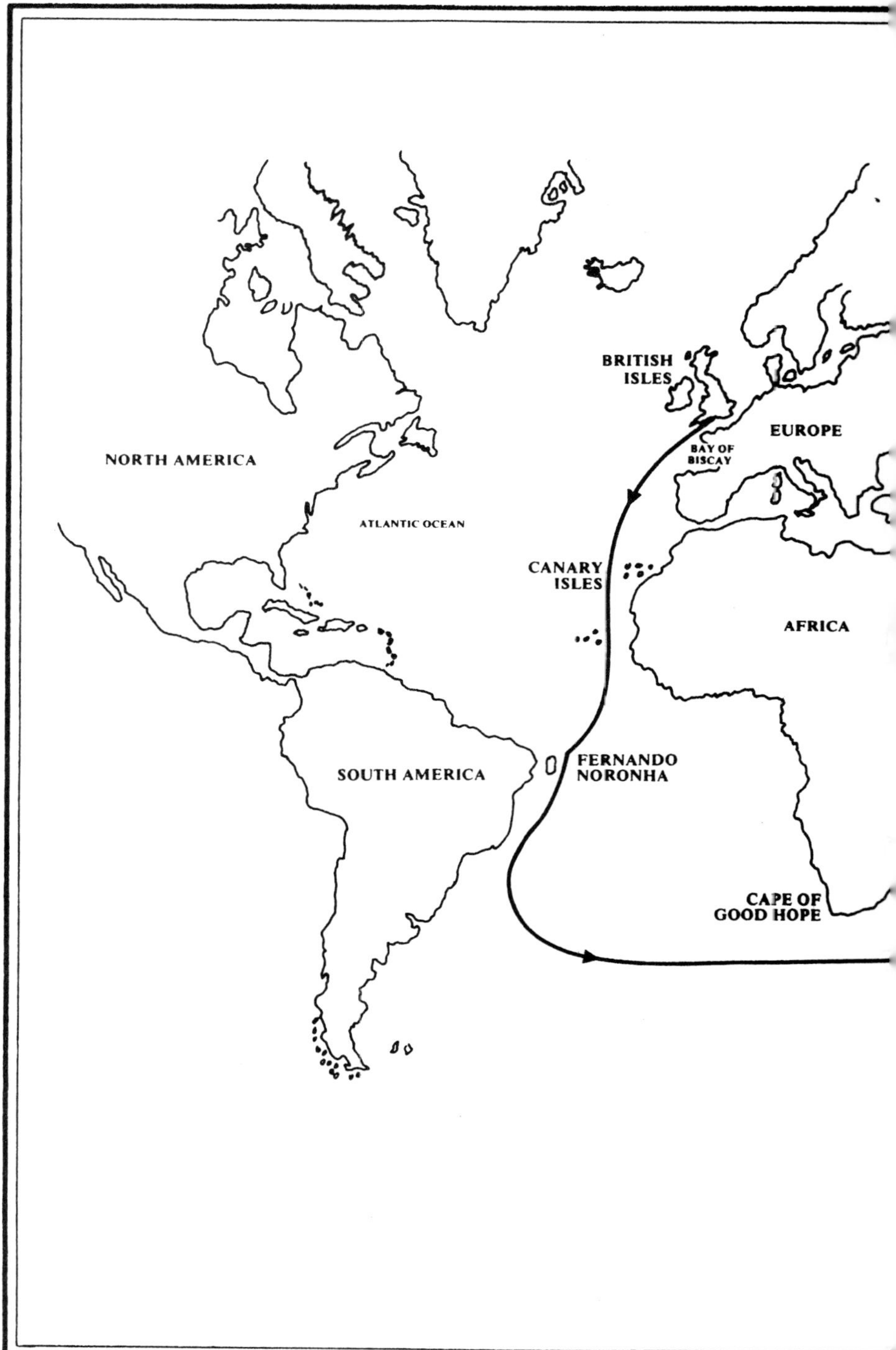
BRITISH ISLES
EUROPE
BAY OF BISCAY
NORTH AMERICA
ATLANTIC OCEAN
CANARY ISLES
AFRICA
FERNANDO NORONHA
SOUTH AMERICA
CAPE OF GOOD HOPE

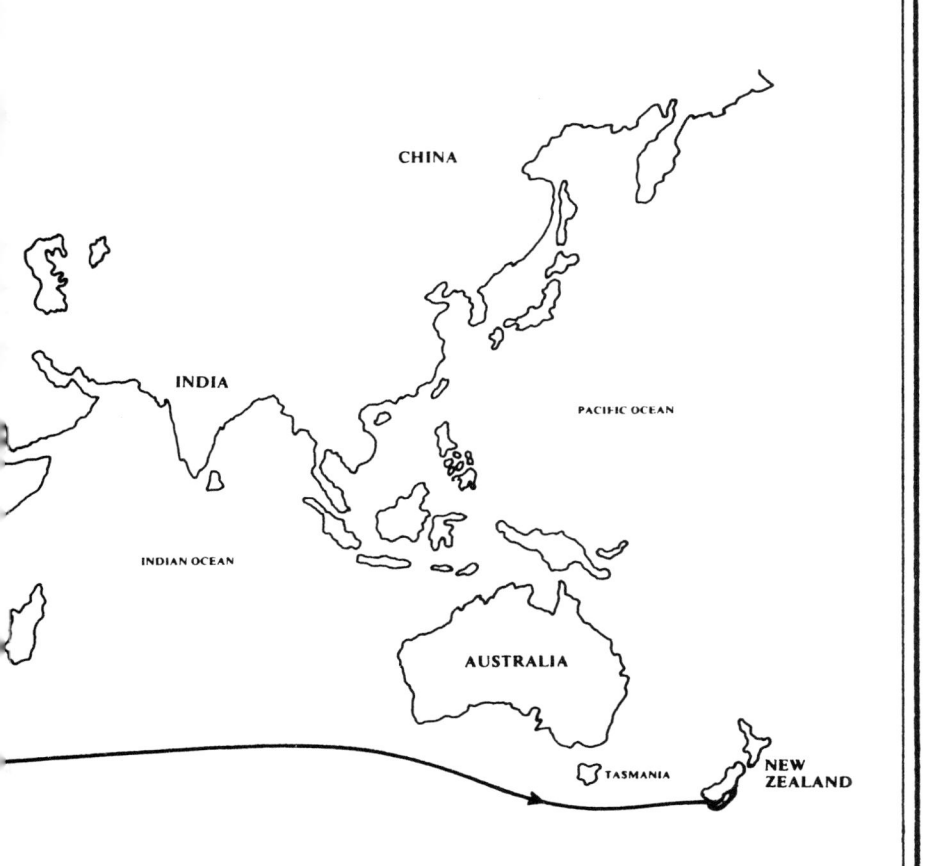

WESTLAND – OUTWARD VOYAGE

NORTH AMERICA

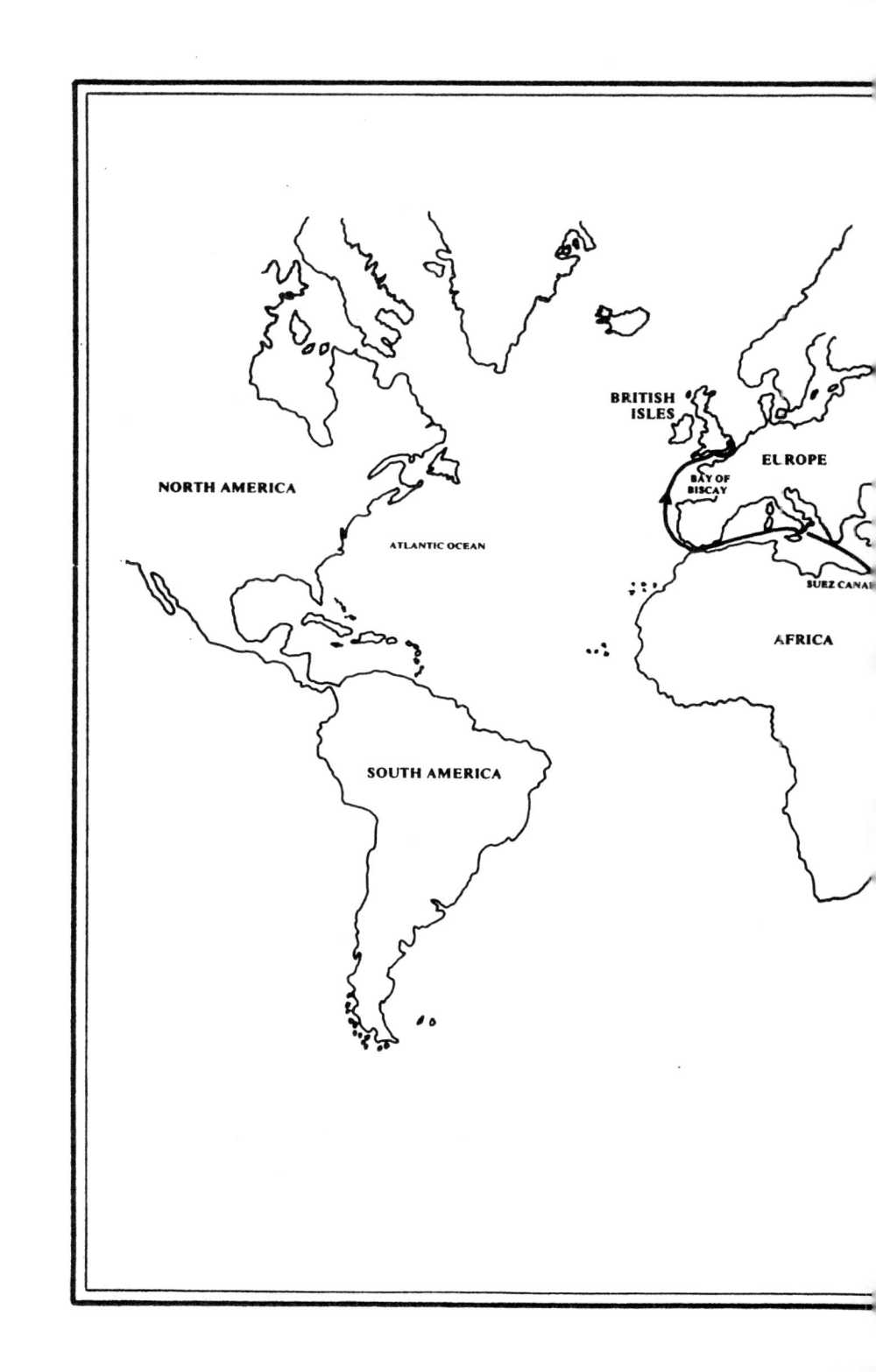

ATLANTIC OCEAN

BRITISH ISLES

EUROPE

BAY OF BISCAY

SUEZ CANAL

AFRICA

SOUTH AMERICA

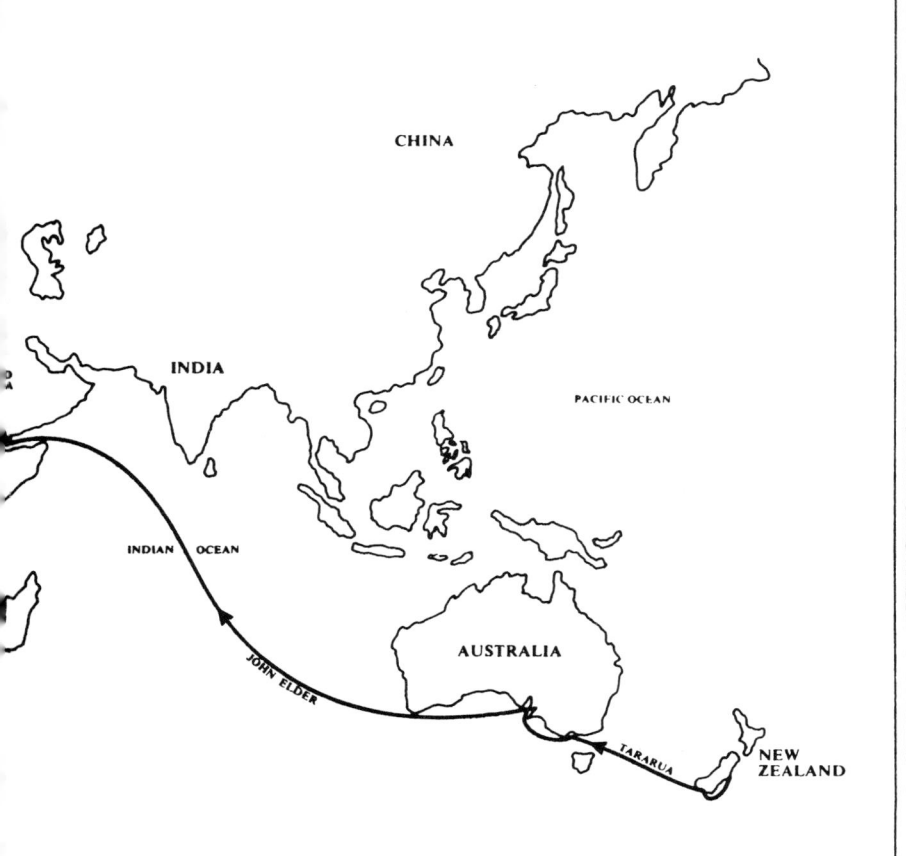

JOHN ELDER – HOMEWARD VOYAGE

Westland

Journal of John Hillary, emigrant to New Zealand, 1879

J.H. Hillary

JANUS PUBLISHING COMPANY
London, England

First published in Great Britain 1979
by Acorn Editions

This edition published in Great Britain 1995
by Janus Publishing Company,
Edinburgh House, 19 Nassau Street,
London W1N 7RE

Copyright © J.H. Hillary 1979, 1995

**British Library Cataloguing-in-Publication Data.
A catalogue record for this book is available from the British Library.**

ISBN 1 85756 109 0

All rights reserved. No part of this publication may be reproduced, stored in a retrieval system or transmitted in any form or by any means, electronic, mechanical, photocopying, recording or otherwise, without the prior permission of the publisher.

The right of J.H. Hillary to be identified as the author of this work has been asserted by him in accordance with the Copyright, Designs and Patents Act 1988.

Printed & bound in England by
Antony Rowe Ltd,
Chippenham, Wiltshire

Contents

	Page
Maps: Outward Voyage	*ii, iii*
Homeward Voyage	*iv, v*
New Zealand	43
List of Illustrations	*xi*
Westland	1
New Zealand	49
Homeward Bound	65
Epilogue	93
Appendix	109

List of Illustrations

Between pages 16 and 17

The 'Westland'
The 'John Elder'
John Hillary
The author

Between pages 48 and 49

The Hillary family: Standing, left to right – Fred, Albert, Herbert. Seated, left to right – Willie, Edith, John Hillary, Mamma, Ethel, John Tom.
View across the Pennines from Tow Law
A page from John Hillary's diary
Dedication page of the Bible given to John Hillary by his Tuesday Bible Class
Dans Castle, Tow Law
Milk delivery, Tow Law

Between pages 80 and 81

The Wesleyan Chapel, Tow Law
The Hillary family pew and commemorative plaque inside the Wesleyan Chapel, Tow Law

To my son, John Hillary — great-grandson of the Diarist

Introduction

In the year 1879 there was touring this country the Rev. J. Berry who would seem to have been an agent for the New Zealand Government. He extolled the virtues of that country and advised people to emigrate to New Zealand and there make their fortunes. John Hillary, a shopkeeper in the small north eastern town of Tow Law, being a deeply religious man, listened to the blandishments of the reverend gentleman and being sure that only truth could come from such a source, decided that as New Zealand must be 'the promised land' he would act upon the advice given.

As many may never have heard of Tow Law I should mention that this is a small town in County Durham and stands astride the A68 – known as the drovers' road. The town, which is over 1,000 ft. above sea level, will be well known to motorists from the South seeking the most direct route to Scotland. Tow Law stands on two hills, the word 'law' in those parts meaning a hill, and 'tow' being the old vernacular for two. It was at that time a lively colliery town in the centre of several coal seams; there were also coke ovens across the fells, and a foundry in the town itself. During recent alterations to London's Underground many old cast iron girders were removed and the name Tow Law was found on them, which mystified many of the workers.

It was from this town that the Hillary family set out on their great adventure. Mother, Father, Willie, John Tom, Albert, Edith, Fred and Baby Herbert, eight persons in all. The ages of the children ranged from the mid-teens down to nine months. John Hillary was a great social worker, local preacher and a very popular person in certain circles. We can imagine that there must have been quite a send off and at that point we join them.

Westland

THE DIARY OF JOHN HILLARY WRITTEN ON THE OCCASION OF HIS JOURNEY WITH HIS FAMILY UNDER SAIL TO NEW ZEALAND. THEIR STAY IN NEW ZEALAND AND THEIR RETURN JOURNEY BY STEAMER.

Friday 21st November, 1879. 'Left Tow Law railway station by the 2.3 p.m. train amidst such expressions of respect as time will never be able to blot from memory's page and after about 4 hours stop at Darlington, and bidding farewell to she who bore me and tenderly raised me from helplessness, after a tedious ride through a cold and stormy night, we arrived at Plymouth about 11 o'clock on Saturday morning.'

While the diarist might have suspected that this could well be the last time he would see his mother alive, he did not realise that she would be dead before the family reached New Zealand. But I will refer to this later. We must at the moment consider their journey through a 'cold and stormy night' probably the longest journey they had ever undertaken, most likely in those days without any heating in the compartment and with six children aged nine months upwards. This was hardly an experience likely to raise their spirits and no doubt feeling decidedly jaded we can understand their reaction to what was to follow.

Saturday 22nd November. 'Were met at the station by an Agent and conducted to the depot where at first sight our hearts almost failed us. Imagine about 300, chiefly Irish and Scotch, many of them of the lowest type, all messing in one room, ten at each table. When mess tickets were given out we ran to the kitchen below for 1½ loaves of bread with a piece of butter on a plate and a can of tea, or if at dinner time a flat brown dish with a partition, having meat on one side and unpeeled potatoes on the other. After mess we had to wash up, wash table down, sweep up crumbs and put forms upon tables and walk out into the enclosed yard, or sit in this one room amidst concertina playing, singing, shouting, whistling, stamping, screaming babies and all the hideous noises by which people could disturb each other, and make the place more like hell. The food was good and plentiful all things considered and the rooms and beds clean, but so narrow were the stalls, the married peoples' being only 3 ft. wide, that it was exceedingly difficult to alter your position during the night or turn over, and for couples of larger proportions I should say impossible. We had to back out feet foremost.'

Sunday 23rd November. 'After breakfast a few others went with me to a splendid new Wesleyan Chapel and heard the Rev. Mr. Banham from Bristol, who was preaching mission sermons. Afternoon we had a walk through the streets of the town and along the quay the weather being beautifully fine. Returning before 5 o'clock we were made prisoners and allowed no more outside the depot walls until we take ship. Emigrants are coming in by every train until the mess room is crowded to suffocation and this horrible place almost unbearable. The Government of England strictly enforces sanitary measures upon its towns and villages, why then is this place not inspected? Four hundred breathing the vitiated air of one room, 100 sleeping in one bedroom, only one stove to which poor starving people can go, and that covered by babies' linen, which mothers are trying in vain to dry, W.C.'s filthy, no comfort. If you go near the stove the arbitrary officials drive you away, indeed the treatment is that of warders to prisoners, civilities are out of the question. The majority of emigrants are of low class and need strict discipline, but there are a number of respectable people who turn from such treatment with tears in their eyes, or looks which say "is Thy servant a dog?" If this place has not sown the seed of disease among these two ships' passengers it will be well.'

How prophetic this last sentence proved to be will be shown later. The Hillary family could not have known at that time just how fortunate they were, for had not the hinge of fate turned ever so slightly and made it necessary, in view of the increased number of emigrants, that an extra vessel had to be chartered, they might well not have lived to see New Zealand.

Monday 24th November. 'This day was employed in examining boxes and was one of confusion. Many having brought feather beds in their luggage had to sell them for a small advance upon nothing. John Payne and family arrived.'

Tuesday 25th November. 'All passed an examination before the doctor in the depot surgery. In the evening the Rev. Mr. Barnes, Chaplain of Plymouth, came and conducted a service and with his Lady's assistance supplied us poor dark emigrants with some tracts. He also considerably diluted his address that it might be adapted to our weak capacities. The Irish made a lot of derisive noises outside. Had a busy afternoon lading all the luggage upon a barge to send down to the ship which is waiting in Plymouth Sound. John Vickers arrived before dinner and got a large share of the hard work.'

This was their last day at the depot, though it does not appear that the diarist was then aware of this. John Hillary does not seem to have appreciated the efforts of the Chaplain of Plymouth to spread the Light of the Gospel, realising no doubt that the Chaplain was probably wasting his time. We must, however, at least commend him for his attempt.

Wednesday 26th November. 'All were ordered to pack up immediately after dinner, and passing in families before the doctor again and receiving contract tickets we walked through the gate to the steamer lying beside the depot wall, and in a short time were put on board the "Westland" in Plymouth Sound. Spent the evening in pacing the deck and singing. We had on board 50 married couples, 55 single men, i.e., over 12 years old, 71 single women, 52 boys under 12, 44 girls, 10 infants, and 36 officers and crew, making a total of 368 souls.'

At last the great day had arrived and the Hillary family must have been greatly relieved to leave the depot behind and to set foot on the 'Westland' and realise that their journey had really begun. The 'Westland' was an iron-hulled ship-rigged vessel built by Robert Duncan & Company of Port Glasgow. She was of the type known as a 'Clipper Ship' being very long and narrow and of the very latest design, being iron-hulled and not of wood construction as had previously been the case. The 'Westland' was approximately 223 ft. long and 35 ft. beam, completed in 1878 and was thus quite new. The Hillarys were fortunate to be travelling in such a fine ship. As we shall see, given favourable conditions, the 'Westland' was capable of quite high speeds and she was of a class built in an attempt to compete with power driven vessels, then coming along in increasing numbers but as we now know an attempt bound to fail in the end. For any reader interested in these tall and graceful ships I have added some further details of the 'Westland' at the end of the book.

We can imagine the scene on board that evening in Plymouth Sound, in my opinion one of the most lovely harbours one could ever find, as they paced the deck singing and with high hopes for the future. This entry always recalls to me the occasion when, as a young man, I first gazed on this lovely stretch of almost landlocked water, surrounded by green hills, and bathed in the light of the setting sun. I looked down from the Hoe and pictured perhaps a similar evening when the 'Westland' lay at anchor with my forbears on board, including my own father.

Thursday 27th November. 'First day on board. All excitement making ready to start. Anchor weighed, during the singing by the sailors of "Goodbye, Farewell etc." and at 12 noon the fine ship "Westland" towed by the steam tug "Secret" started her long and perilous voyage to the Antipodes. Passed the Eddystone Lighthouse and very soon the breeze catching our ship the tug was no longer needed. We one after another began to feel "Oh! my," and hurried to our bunks below all drunk without drink. When I got down the hatchway I said "Kind friends, I'm feeling very queer", and was soon into my bed. Had a rough night, and were most of us very sick. The constables came round with slop pails and another utensil which I shall not more minutely describe than by saying it resembled in shape "grandfather's hat". These utensils were soon in great demand. Cries and groans proceeded from all sides, not only from the children but from strong men and women as though caught by a terrible panic or epidemic; others lay still as pallid as death.'

Friday 28th November. (First day's sail of 24 hrs.) 296 miles. 'We all spent this day in bed being very sick and ill, Mamma and Edith especially so. We are now in the Bay of Biscay and are experiencing heavy weather. Many who had long neglected now lifted their voices to Him who "calms the roaring seas" for protection. The ship rolls and pitches fearfully, seas break over her and quantities of water come pouring down the hatchways. The few who can keep up are kept very busy ministering to the wants of the sufferers who are thankful for a drop of cold water. Some are very ill, their upheavals being distressing to hear. "Barney", cries a big Irishman, "she's going down". "Let her go", responds the other, "I don't care where she goes, I'm dying". "Dennis, fetch here a bucket", cries another, "for I'm vomitting my pluck". "Jim", cries a woman in the next bunk to ours, "we are going down this time, Lord have mercy on us". The hatchways are covered with tarpaulin to keep the seas out, and the effluvia between decks on account of the sickness is becoming very unpleasant."

Saturday 29th November. (Second day) 306 miles. 'After a terrible night about 6 am we passed out of the Bay which has been the awful destruction of so many gallant ships and the winding sheet of so many emigrants not the least the Rev D.J. Draper of the "London". Whiting and I lifted up our hearts to God in thankfulness for His mercy. Are doing 13 knots per hour with a strong side wind and the sea is very tempestuous. The sailors say we have already done as much as some vessels have done in 23 days and are promising to make a very quick passage. A quarter to 4 pm, sighted a French ship which being lightly laden is fearfully tossed by the furious waves. Sometimes she seems almost swallowed up and gone then she rises like a cork and is upheaved almost to the clouds. Those on deck are holding on to anything they can seize for life. Many of our adult passengers are still very sick and also many of the children. Doctor Russell has a busy time of it. Mrs. H. being helpless I have had to wash some of the baby linen this evening. Mrs. C. Neill has presented her husband with a baby while coming through the Bay it is named Westland after the ship.'

Our travellers had an early baptism and were soon experiencing very stormy weather and one can realise from these entries something of what 'crossing the Bay' must have meant in those days. What the diarist is describing would today have been considered a scene of horror. Bear in mind that the 'Westland' was never designed as a passenger vessel and that these people were actually accommodated in the hold intended solely for the stowage of cargo. Already wind-jammers were hard pressed to obtain freight and there was a lucrative business to be done in the carriage of emigrants to New Zealand and wool etc. on the return voyage. To this end collapsible bunks were fitted in the cargo holds, as many as possible, with only a curtain between for privacy.

Consider what these conditions must have been like in the extremely stormy weather the vessel was now experiencing – the hatches battened down to prevent the sea water coming down below, because the decks would be completely awash. No air conditioning, in fact very little ventilation of any sort, and with everyone sick the stench must have been appalling. Particularly during the night when the only light available would be from a few early type oil lamps, with the sea crashing on deck and pounding against the hull, the noise and darkness would have been terrifying to any traveller today. But the Victorians were pretty tough and we must admire the women who went on board knowing that they must 'deliver' before the voyage was ended. Even Mrs Hillary had six children to contend with

WESTLAND

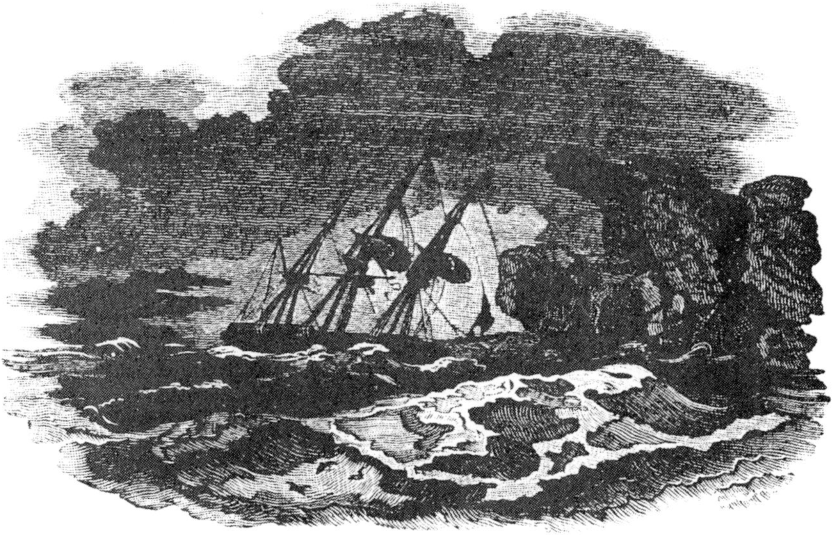

including a child in arms – no wonder a little Westland arrived under these conditions. However our diarist writes quite calmly and does not himself seem unduly alarmed.

A point of interest during the last two days is the mileage run, 296 miles the first day and 306 the second, a total of 602 miles in 48 hours. Not bad going under sail, and much better than most steamers could manage at that time. This 306 miles was the best day's sailing of the voyage, but the 'Westland' frequently exceeded this figure on other occasions.

Sunday 30th November. (Third day) 263 miles. 'Beautiful morning and a fine breeze. Sighted another ship about noon. Making rapid progress all much improved in health. The wonders of "The great deep profound" this marvellous apocalypse of God shut my mouth and fill me with reverent awe. Like the psalmist I cry out "Oh Lord etc" Psalm 104. Feel a longing for the habitation of God's House, depressed because I cannot keep Holy Day with His people.'

Monday 1st December. (Fourth day) 238 miles. 'The roughest day we have had and people sick on all sides some seriously ill. Ship rolls fearfully. Our family are all bad excepting little Fred who is the best sailor. I am obliged to move about and being so dizzy have had two nasty falls on deck. Mamma says when she writes home she will dissuade anyone intending coming but I suppose this is another of the speeches women make in haste to rue in their leisure. A weeks rations given out in the messes.'

Tuesday 2nd December. (Fifth day) 158 miles. 'After a rough night the storm is but slightly abated. People with wry faces are sitting about on deck evidently very feeble. Passed a ship going in the same direction but not nearly so fast. Scarlet fever has already made its appearance among the children. Are bringing all our beds on deck for an airing. Berths are very close and warm.'

After a lull on November 30th, more stormy weather for two days; 'Ship rolls fearfully' says the diarist and this would be the case. No stabilizers were fitted to this vessel, and with three great heavy wooden masts, each well over 100 ft. high, together with a narrow beam, clippers were noted rollers under certain conditions. No wonder John Hillary had two falls on deck; he would be by no means the only one.

Wednesday 3rd December. (Sixth day) 228 miles. 'A beautiful day and all on deck enjoying the sea breeze, much improved. Sighted the island of Teneriffe which is 12,336 ft above sea level. Remained on deck until after 11 pm.'

Thursday 4th December. (Seventh day) 64 miles. 'Are this morning about the same place we were last night, with Teneriffe Peak before us and a contrary wind. Are making no progress. Am told ships are becalmed sometimes here for a week.'

Friday 5th December. (Eighth day) 47 miles. 'Are still dodging about the coast of Teneriffe this morning. A small Spanish schooner passed us this afternoon and we signalled and spoke her. Also sighted two other ships. All recovering. At eventide were favoured with some propitious wind and got away. At 10 pm are going about 7 knots and passing the last of the Canary Islands. John Tom while looking over the ship's side had his hat struck off his head by a rope and it was lost.'

Teneriffe is the largest of the Canary Islands, the peak of Teneriffe being the highest of this volcanic group, today much visited by tourists. Note here the day's run of only 47 miles, the lowest so far. One of the old 'Steam kettles' could catch them up now, and in those days it was often the tale of the hare and the tortoise. It was the reliability of steam that was beginning to tell; steamers could deliver cargoes on time, sail could not, even if on occasions it was quicker. Later with increased engine power even this advantage was lost.

Saturday 6th December. (Ninth day) 105 miles. 'Are going well. Had a death on board and a burial. We never knew of her illness until startled by the news of her death, we skinned and threw the body overboard mourning only the loss of the mutton. While I was writing this afternoon John Tom walked up with two fruit loaves of his own making, his Mamma laughed heartily at them. Willie is busy making a pudding for Sunday's dinner. The provisions are good both in quality and quantity, excepting the bread which on account of the heat is rather sour. Weather beautifully fine and sunny and we can hardly realise the fact that Christmas is so close upon us and yet we are apparently in midsummer.'

Sunday 7th December. (Tenth day) 203 miles. 'Passed a brig this morning and hoisted the British flag which was replied to, and a conversation went on for some time between the captains by means of the ensigns. In the morning Dr. Russell read the church service on deck and in the evening I was requested to preach, which I did from "If ye being evil etc". Just as I had got to the marrow of my discourse Captain Wood came to tell me he was very sorry to interrupt us but the ship was out of her course and would have to be turned. We had therefore to break up abruptly. Weather very warm especially so at night. We can scarcely bear it in bed even without covering. Having no wind we are almost standing still tonight.'

Monday 8th December. (Eleventh day) 39 miles. 'No wind and doing little. Week's rations served out also a supply of lime juice. This tropical heat is intense being 146 degrees in the cook and bakehouse. Quite a stir on board on account of greybacks having made their appearance on the outside clothing of some Irishmen. Doctor ordered their beds to be brought on deck and searched about eight times, and had their persons stripped and scrubbed in a large tub of water and disinfectants behind a screen. A great treat was afforded us in the evening, witnessing the gorgeous beauty of an eastern sunset of which I had heard so much, but it beggars all description. Often think of friends at home and wish I could entertain them an hour by a recital of what I have already experienced.'

An eventful day, although the diarist was quite unaware of this. Only one person fully appreciated the significance of the situation and that was the ship's doctor – Dr. Russell – who acted with great promptness and thoroughness. It is only true to say that his quick appraisal of the position probably saved many lives. How fortunate were the passengers and crew to have on board a man of such quick perception and, as we shall see throughout the voyage, devotion to duty. It is rather surprising that John Hillary, a man of intelligence, did not realise why it was necessary to have these lice-infested beds searched so many times and the bodies of the persons involved scrubbed and disinfected so thoroughly. Had he realised the significance of the event he would not have treated the subject so lightly.

Tuesday 9th December. (Twelfth day) 50 miles. 'Weather lovely but rather too warm. Had a grand concert on deck tonight, the passengers and crew going through a lengthy programme in good style. Dr. Russell presided and Captain Wood led off with the "The Sexton" as first song. This was a relief to the monotony of sea life to those whose tastes were in that line, but, oh how I thought of my class at home assembled in a better cause, and longed to be with them.'

Wednesday 10th December. (Thirteenth day) 118 miles. 'Weather very warm. Are now in the tropics and have had another supply of lime juice. Going about 6 knots per hour. Saw a lot of flying fish today and one alighting upon deck was an object of much interest to the passengers. They are a little larger than a herring and very pretty, fly about 50 yards at once and then return to the water. I was watchman from 4 to 7 this morning and just as I came on duty another little "Westland" was added to our number (Tarling). Am thankful he did not come to our berth for I have quite plenty to look after. Are not sorry that the Shaw Savill & Company's "Trevelyan" had not discharged her grain cargo in time, and that the Company had to charter Pat Henderson & Company's "Westland" for us, as she is such a good sailor, so roomly between decks, and the provisions are so plentiful that we cannot use them all. We have fresh bread daily and fresh water. Milk (condensed) twice and preserved meat once for the children daily. Weekly we receive loaf and moist sugar, butter, flour, suet, raisins, rice, oatmeal, pickles, carrots, onions, soup, pepper, salt and mustard, preserved meat, salt beef and pork, also porridge (burgon) every morning. We often have to refuse taking articles as our tins are full. We can have anything we make cooked in a few minutes, and many are living better on ship than they did at home. Ship is (I am told) provisioned for eight months.'

Thursday 11th December. (Fourteenth day) 147 miles. 'This was a busy day taking the wanted baggage out of the hold and opening our boxes, putting away all our heavy clothing and taking light clothes out suitable for the weather. Our children were well pleased with the apples and oranges Uncle kindly put in for them, and their father was not less pleased to get his field-glass and fiddle out, but especially the box of fragrant weed sent him by Messrs. Harvey & Davy, which smoked so well. The loaf of "brown geordie" was moulded, and jam and marmalade split in the box bottom, but thanks to the liberality of the New Zealand Government we had no want. My glass was an object of much interest and many were anxious to know where I had come from, and what I had been to receive such tokens of respect. Am told by several I should do well in N.Z., but that is all to try yet.'

A busy day indeed – how pleased they must have been to get into thinner clothing as they approached the Equator. Even the lighter clothing would have been considered quite thick by modern standards. The ladies with skirts and several petticoats at least to the ankles, and more intimate garments down to the knees. The men would normally have worn long pants and vests even in summer, with shirts to the neck and wrists; shorts were of course quite unknown. The heat of the tropics was to change all this for the men, but not for the ladies, I fear. We note a mention of 'brown geordie', this merely being a loaf of brown bread. 'My glass' was the telescope bought for the diarist by the members of his bible class which, if the reader has not already gathered, met every Tuesday evening, and will be mentioned frequently. Apart from the pubs, to which John Hillary would not go, this 'class' seems to have represented his weekly entertainment.

Friday 12th December. (Fifteenth day) 154 miles. 'Nothing particular to report excepting that the heat gradually increases as we near the Equator, especially do we suffer from it at night while in bed. Many passengers are unwell on this account.

Sighted a large vessel near us and got a good view of her with the glass.'

Saturday 13th December. (Sixteenth day) 140 miles. 'School commenced this morning. Several porpoises seen near our ship. Are becoming quite adapted to "a life on the ocean wave", and forming friendships. Have got our sea legs and can trot about on deck easily. Often think how our friends at home will fear that every gale they experience now will affect us, little knowing what a beautiful mild climate we are in, and how, when a little gale does arise the noble "Westland" laughs it to scorn, and proudly rides over the angry billows of the restless sea. How dark our friends are about a sea voyage, and so were we until we got this experience. Could I sit down one evening at home I think with what breathless silence they would listen to me for two or three hours.'

Just over two weeks aboard, very steady sailing, 140 miles per day under pleasant conditions. My grandmother, 'Mamma', used to tell me when I was a boy, that under these conditions there was, when below, no sense of movement. The only means of knowing whether progress was being made was to look out of one of the portholes and see the water going by. There was, of course, no engine noise, and no doubt by this time our travellers were so used to any slight movement of the ship as not to notice it. The diarist is here in good spirits, all memories of crossing the Bay having been forgotten.

Sunday 14th December. (Seventeenth day) 79 miles. 'A beautiful morning. We spent a restless night on account of the heat, the thermometer registering 85 in the berths. We mustered at 10 am for the service; after calling the roll the Captain sent for me and asked me to preach as Dr. Russell felt himself unable to read the service. We had a good company, and I addressed them from "The Great Supper" – Luke 14. The Skipper seemed to enjoy it and spoke very favourably to me. Afternoon we sighted not less than 5 ships, one of them being a magnificent steamer. I took out my glass (thanks to my class) and was surrounded by people asking for a look, we had a splendid view. This eventful day closed with the death of our last accession, baby No.2, and a grand tropical thunderstorm. Talk of lightning, well, the heavens opened and the electric fluid lighted the sea up for miles and played and quivered upon the ship, awfully grand, and to say it rained is no description, for the waters above the firmament seemed to join those of the sea. The sailors enjoyed it very much.'

Monday 15th December. (Eighteenth day) 127 miles. 'The infant's remains were early this morning quietly added to the vast number who, at the last blast of the "archangel's trumpet" shall arise from the mighty deep. Sugar, tea, rice, oatmeal, butter, etc. are accumulating and I cannot find room to bestow all my goods, as the cannisters are all full. After dark we sighted a fine steamer passing us at about 8 miles distance, with my glass I could see the lights in her cabins.'

Tuesday 16th December. (Nineteenth day) 83 miles. 'Sighted 5 ships in the morning, but all were a good distance off us. The heat is so intense I slept on deck last night. Joined my class in spirit, at the time I thought they would be assembled, but this is difficult to ascertain as the ship's time is taken from the sun and is almost 2 hours behind London time. Felt a great need of spiritual fellowship and private prayer, no opportunities being afforded. Making very little progress.'

Wednesday 17th December. (Twentieth day) 53 miles. 'Sighted 3 ships, and my glass was highly spoken of by judges, but am wearied with the number of people wanting a look every time it is out. Had one of natures grandest panoramas in a splendid sunset, which baffles my descriptive powers, as it would also the limner's skill, its beauties we shall never forget. Another concert on deck this evening, when a lady sang "Far Away" very touchingly, and was especially so to us under existing circumstances.'

'My glass' is proving to be a not unmixed blessing. Perhaps some readers may have found themselves in a similar position, and while it is amusing to read about, one must have some sympathy for the diarist. The use of the word 'limner' for a painter is interesting and would not be used today. The concert

The 'Westland'

The 'John Elder'

John Hillary

The author

seems almost to have been enjoyed, but then this was not a Tuesday evening.

Thursday 18th December. (Twentyfirst day) 92 miles. 'Three vessels in view when I came on deck before 6 am. It is said one of them left London about the same time as us, but Mr. Phillips, the first mate, says when we get the wind she will soon be left behind, for the "Westland" can beat all competitors with a good wind. As every man's horse is the best so must sailors crack off their own ship but I find from statistics Mr. Phillips' statement is borne out by the passages she has made. Some curious little fish swarm close to the ship's side today, about four inches in length and resembling a toy boat. They are named Argonauts but the sailors call them Portuguese Men of War. Sometimes whole fleets of them may be seen sailing past with their purple sails up and rowing swiftly with their tentacula or feelers out, but on being approached in go the tentacula and down sinks the miniature sail as the fish concentrates itself into its shell and both vanish together like a fairy of the sea. Quite a commotion on deck today one of the single men having been robbed of two pounds his whole capital. I think a stowaway among the sailors will know something about it. Dr. Russell posted up a notice that cash or valuables could be deposited with him up to the end of the voyage. Almost all of us embraced the opportunity. Heat almost unbearable, thermometer registering 86 in the berths and 140 in the bake and cookhouse. Many are struck-out with the scarlet rash, prickly heat and suffering from diarrhoea.'

It was of course very natural for the 1st mate to feel proud of the 'Westland' but she did prove to be a fast ship and achieved many quick passages. It is on record that on one occasion she was the last of a fleet of 20 ships to leave New Zealand in the wool season. Yet she arrived back in England 22 days before any of the other vessels. The 'Westland' was in fact loaded and ready to sail out again when the first of the fleet the 'Wairoa', a fully rigged ship, reached London after a very respectable voyage of 91 days.

Friday 19 December. (Twentysecond day) 86 miles. 'All beds and bedding on deck this morning having the parasites brushed off them, of course I refer to the Flannagans and the McFaratys many of whom are getting to be very lively. Mothers are all busy washing and we fathers are of course busier nursing. Oh the joys of married life.'

Saturday 20th December. (Twentythird day) 76 miles. 'The Dr. put me on the dicky brigade this morning, the beds and bedding being all brought on deck and searched. On the whole they were very clean but we found a few alive and several dead skins on the beds of some of the Irish people. This day towards its close was a most eventful one. The sailors were on the ship a week before the passengers and as the wage is for them to receive a months salary in advance on signing articles this was the end of it. The end of the first month is with them always a time of rejoicing for as they term it they have been working for a dead horse and now their wages begin to accumulate. They celebrate the event by making a sham horse and stuffing him with straw, tar, pitch or any bituminous substances and placing him upon the wheel of the gun. They paint black or mask their faces put on the most ridiculous cockades, long rope whiskers, white skirts or red coats. One of them being seated astride the horse having an effigy of a wife and baby behind is drawn by the others as with lighted torches in their hands and headed by a flag they procession the deck singing as only sailors can sing and playing sackbut, flute, tin whistle, tin can and all kinds of music. On arrival at the Captain's cabin door one of them dressed the most ridiculously holding up a large wooden mallet turns auctioneer and after calling the sale by a trumpet, sells his horse to the highest bidder. A collection is then made and everything being pre-arranged horse and rider are drawn up to the yard-arm when the sailor rider strikes the horse a blow in the side with his knife striking fire, he then cuts the rope letting the burning horse drop into the sea while the rider very cleverly holds to the yard-arm and is lowered down to the deck. The burning horse can be seen for a great distance. This affairs ends as usual by the sailors assembling at the Captain's cabin and each being served with a glass of the best "O be joyful". The days proceedings were ended by a concert under the poop over which Captain Wood presided and at which Mr. Phillips (1st mate) sang "They all get married but me" Mr. Lesly (2nd mate) sang "Rule Britannia" and several of the sailors sang good songs. Sailors have fine voices. The heat is so intense I mostly sleep on deck at nights. Some lie in the boats but the rats are very numerous there.'

The doctor is still keeping a firm hold on the lice situation. The account of the celebration on board is most interesting and detailed, and could well be unique as the writer has never heard of this event before. It is a matter of interest that there is no account of any celebration when crossing the line a few days later. There is no mention of this on the homeward journey either. It is interesting to note that a gun was carried even at that time.

Sunday 21st December (Twentyfourth day) 41 miles. 'Mustered for roll-call and service at 10 am. Prayers read by Dr. Russell. A nice dish of stew of my making for dinner and a fruit cake of Mamma's making for tea. In the evening we spent some time sitting on the forecastle watching a passing ship and enjoying the cooling sea breeze. Was pained to hear the look-out man who is an old sailor of superior education stuffing some green Irishmen with big fish stories of what he had seen and done during his seafaring life. The dear boys with eyes and mouths wide open were taking all in as truth and seeing this he did pile it on. Old Joe is a notorious liar for as a messmate of ours from Leeds observed he is quite ahead of "Tom Pepper" and he was two degrees beyond the Devil.'

Monday 22nd December (Twentyfifth day) 89 miles. 'Most of this day was occupied in giving out our weekly provisions and thanks to the liberality of the Provincial Government in addition to our dietary scales supply we had extras given for making our Xmas Plum Pudding. We think, however, we should have relished our Xmas dinner better beside a warm fire in old England than under the scorching rays of a tropical sun. In the evening we spoke of a French Barque. There are a few glasses on board but thanks to my class mine is declared the best. At night I was on the first watch 10 pm to 1 am, and the rats were running in all directions, I saw seven. The sailors say they are quite harmless only nibbling their toe nails or the horned parts of the soles of their feet.'

The provisions seem to have been very good indeed and the diarist makes no complaints on that score. For emigrants the supplies seem to have been both good in quality and quantity. The writer was under the impression that emigrants paid almost nothing for their passage. It is interesting to learn that Shaw Savills secured the contract for emigrants to New Zealand in 1863, fares being £12 from Glasgow and £13.10s from London. If this means per person then John Hillary with his family must have paid a fair amount and if one multiplies this by ten we can obtain a very rough idea of how much this would be today. It seems strange that one can emigrate to Australia by air today for far less, pro rata, than the diarist paid. It must, however be remembered that the journey today takes only a matter of hours whereas the Hillary family had to be housed and fed for three months.

Tuesday 23rd December. (Twentysixth day) 32 miles. 'This morning the French vessel is still lying by us and a large ship meeting us returning from San Francisco to Queenstown. We are almost becalmed which I suppose is very usual in these parts any little wind being of short duration. In this is seen the advantage of a steamer over a wind ship. The hopes of the officials of making this a sharp voyage seem to be almost abandoned and unless when we get over the line much improvement is made our voyage will be tediously long and we shall know how to esteem the comforts of a home again, be it ever so humble.'

Wednesday 24th December. (Twentyseventh day) 105 miles. 'One month over in safety thank God. Busy making plum pudding and Xmas cakes. Captain Wood has kindly given a small piece of cheese and Dr. Russell a bottle of stout to each family. We receive many kindnesses from the head officials but on the other hand have to endure many incivilities from the subbordinates and to complain is to our hurt for bullying and cursing seems to be the rule here, however we shall have an opportunity of stating our grievances at the end of the voyage. The supply of food is liberal beyond our expectations but made ready so roughly that much of it is wasted and stones of bread go overboard. A beautiful moonlight Xmas eve and so hot that many do not intend going down to their berths but will sleep on deck.'

Thursday Xmas Day. (Twentyeighth day) 80 miles. 'The birthday of the world's Redeemer and mine. While the thoughtless are carrying on sports on deck in the form of three legged races, jumping etc I am meditating on that peerless mystery of Divine love in Christ Jesus. Was sorry to see Xmas day so recklessly spent by Captain and crew but a large proportion of the passengers are Scotch who pay more regard to New Years Day. It was a great change to us spending Xmas day where the heat is so intense that the pitch in the joints of the deck floorboards boiled out. Thought much of our friends, how they would be employed and what fare they would be having. For their information I may say we had beef, potatoes, plum pudding with brandy sauce, fruit cake, toffee for the children and a glass of whisky for the fathers who like to take it, surely this is not bad fare for emigrants on board ship. On account of the heat at night I left my bed and came on deck but the heavy rain compelling me to return below, I sat down on the hatchway stairs and fell asleep. I was awoke by a large rat sitting on the back of my neck and did not lose much time in shaking him off. He clung to the steps with his claws like a strong kitten. We think little of this having got so accustomed to them running over us in bed and playing round the deck.'

The writer was, when young, to celebrate quite a few Christmases at John Hillary's home, and it is interesting to contrast this entry with later events. The diarist always insisted that the grandchildren, now fairly numerous, should eat Christmas dinner at a separate table and in another room to their parents. John Hillary would then produce his fiddle, the one mentioned in the diary, and while we children were eating he would play tunes likely to appeal to the younger taste, nursery rhymes etc. How different this Christmas must have been, in the heat of the tropics compared with the cold of Tow Law, which can be quite severe as anyone knowing the district will agree. As a matter of fact, Christmas dinner was not John Hillary's favourite meal; he much preferred his giblet pie supper, when all the grandchildren were safely tucked in bed. Even if he was one of the fathers who refused a tot of whisky, it is difficult to see how he avoided the brandy in the sauce.

Friday 26th December. (Twentyninth day) 64 miles. 'Crossed the Equator during the night and were at noon today 12 miles east of it. Several large porpoises near the ship. They resemble a boat sailing bottom uppermost, and their broad backs rise and fall with the regularity of a ship.'

Saturday 27th December. (Thirtieth day) 129 miles. 'Having got fairly into the South Atlantic we have caught the south east trade winds and are going along in splendid style. The sea runs high and tosses the ship very much. Mrs. H. having gone down stairs to make a cake for tomorrows tea had a recurrence of sickness. Several are sick again today. Spoke to a ship named "Mary Stuart" from Swansea to Bolivia in South America.'

Sunday 28th December. (Thirtyfirst day) 214 miles. 'This morning sighted two vessels and passed very near the island Fernando Noronha, a penal settlement owned by Brazil, it is 7 miles long by 2½ miles wide. With my glass I could see houses, roads, fields and trees, and in an aperture between the rocks a landscape resembling some of the Weardale scenes; was to me one of the greatest treats, for after a months view of the sea and sky only, the sight of green fields was good for sore eyes. After muster Captain asked me to take the service which I declined, because when prayers are read by the Dr, all seem to attend as a duty but when we few dissenters hold a preaching service people don't seem to feel under any obligation to come and the under-officials go on dealing out water, bread, meat and doing whatever they can to interupt what they consider to be a put-off service. I am anxious to do what good I can and after the kindness of Dr, and Captain sorry to refuse but it is possible to make yourself too cheap, to cast pearls before swine and by an injuditious use of religion to bring it into contempt. Read a few psalms which greatly refreshed my soul but the depth of the longing I felt for the Sanctuary of God my pen could ne'er express.'

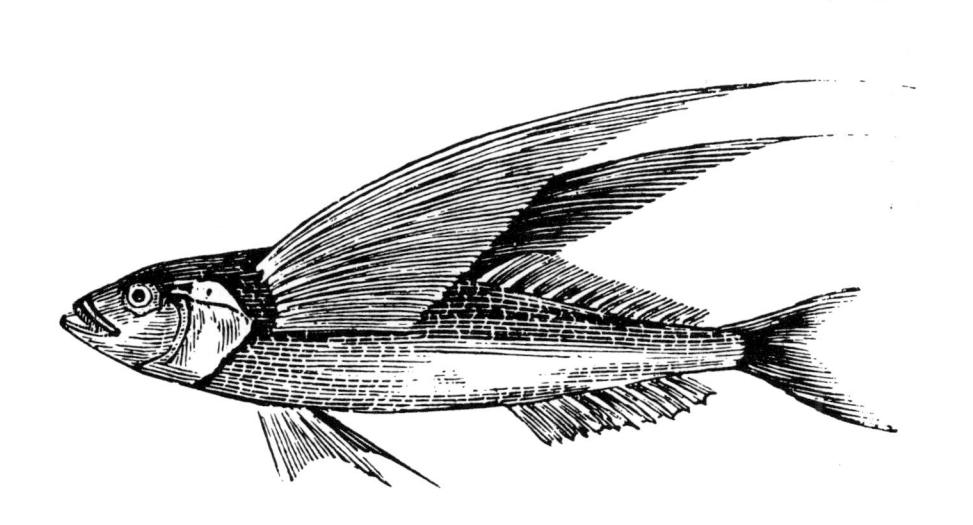

WESTLAND

Strange as it may seem the 'Westland' had not been following the coasts of Spain and West Africa but as we see was now close to the coast of Brazil in South America, having thus crossed the Atlantic Ocean. This put a considerable mileage on the journey and they were to follow the coast of Brazil for several days before turning East towards New Zealand. This detour was of course not without reason and was to catch the Easterlies and the Roaring Forties, winds which blew fairly constantly along the 40th parallel and along which they were to sail for several thousand miles, passing the Cape of Good Hope where Cape Town stands. After turning East we will see the daily mileages rising again as for some time now they had been sailing in the area of the Doldrums noted for lack of wind and where ships have been known to be becalmed for weeks.

They were very lucky really to have made the journey so quickly. They had already one month on board and had another two months to endure before reaching their destination. One can quite understand how the diarist felt at seeing green fields again. The writer well remembers, in recent times, a relative writing when on a voyage to South Africa, prefacing her letter with the words 'Nothing to see but the bloody ocean'. After leaving the coast of Brazil our travellers would see no more land for another eight weeks so they were destined to see a great deal of the 'bloody ocean' before reaching New Zealand.

It is interesting to note that today the journey by sea to New Zealand is still made by crossing the Atlantic but then via the Panama Canal into the Pacific. There was at that time no Panama Canal though the first abortive attempts at construction were to be made in the following year, 1880. The canal was, however, not finally completed before the beginning of this century. The Suez Canal had been in use for about 10 years already but this was of no use to sailing ships.

Monday 29th December. (Thirtysecond day) 197 miles. 'Are 44 miles from the coast of South America. A busy day giving out weekly supplies. This is the first time in my life when I could live and keep out of debt without money, yet have stores coming in weekly plenty to eat and no bills to meet. Had a view of the coast of Brazil, could see the trees by the aid of my glass and six coasting ships. In the evening while lying on the forecastle one of these coasting smacks passed us at speaking distance on our port side and we exchanged a shout of recognition.'

Tuesday 30th December. (Thirtythird day) 136 miles. 'Having little wind the heat is terrible. Our day dress is approaching the primeval our night-dress being almost quite so. The nights bring little relief on account of the air being so hot in these parts. Mrs. H. says my friends will little think that on Xmas week I am trotting about the deck with nothing on but straw hat, shirt and trousers, minus both stockings and boots. Three ships passed this afternoon and one a steamer at night. Thermometer stood at 86 in the berths at 11.pm. Captain put a man on look-out this morning with as many eyes in his face as there are days in this year. I suppose he will keep us off the rocks. During the night had another accession to our numbers a "gal" this must be put a stop to we cannot have passengers or rather stow-aways coming on in this way without either paying their passage or being nominated.'

Wednesday 31st December. (Thirtyfourth day) 145 miles. 'About 7.am. the "Market Castle" of Boston, a three masted schooner passed so close to us that we could clearly see the people on her deck with the naked eye. Fearfully hot great preparation being made for New Years Day. Mrs. H. is just busy making toffee, ginger bread cakes etc. Could our friends but see the set-out at the cookhouse, their ideas of poor fare on an emigrant ship would be corrected. Thought much about the rapid flight of time, the Watch Night service which would have been my thirty-third in the old chapel and lastly how, if at home, I should have been friend M.G. Barrows' "Lucky Bird", and with a few friends comfortably seated round his festive table telling stories, and trying to increase the joy of his guests. Had I been there this year, however, my recitals would have had an unusual interest for them.'

Thursday 1st January 1880. (Thirtyfifth day) 219 miles. 'A New Year has come to all, young and old, poor and rich, the cottage and the hall. Usual congratulations exchanged on deck this morning, and as we are all leaving Britain for one reason and this year will be an epoch in the life of each, we hoped it might be one of the brightest and best. Going at a rapid pace, we are many of us poorly today and unfit to eat anything. The day closed with a concert of secular songs. This is a godless place, and there is such an attempt to blend light and darkness, as well try to mix fire and water. Captain Wood asks me to preach on the Sabbath, and himself reads the lessons, yet during the week he sings songs, leads off the dance, allows much profane swearing among his crew, and himself sets the example. Gather not my soul with sinners, nor my life with bloody men.'

It is necessary at this stage to prevent a wrong impression being created in the mind of the reader concerning the type of man the diarist really was. He was by no means a sour, thin faced individual, pacing the deck with a telescope under one arm and a bible under the other, preaching hell fire. He was a short man of very cheery disposition, always ready for a joke and with a ready smile. In later life he always wore a smoking cap, but it is doubtful if this was the case at the time of the voyage. He was by now a teetotaller, though he had not by any means always been so, but he was a pipe smoker and this he remained for the rest of his life.

To understand the position clearly it is necessary to appreciate the conditions then pertaining. John Hillary lived in an age of religious revival, churches and chapels were full and hell fire preached and believed in. The population was divided between the religious and the irreligious, and in the former there was a tremendous puritanical streak which ran through the Victorians generally. As any reader of the literature of the times will be aware they were reputedly great people for falling on their knees and thanking God for any blessing which they imagined they had received. One has only to read such books as 'John Halifax Gentleman', 'Tom Brown's School Days' and that classic of priggishness 'Pilgrim's Progress' to gain some idea of the atmosphere surrounding the upbringing of many people at that time. It may be the Victorians embraced religion because they feared to go to Hell, but they were very fervent in their beliefs and decidedly intolerant of others who did not share their views. John Hillary was no different from thousands of people of his generation, and despite his sanctimonious views was at heart a good and kindly man ever ready to give help where needed.

It is perhaps difficult for the younger reader to comprehend fully conditions as they were nearly one hundred years ago. Life consisted largely of work for long hours under shocking conditions, which would not be tolerated today. For most people there were only two ways of alleviating their sufferings, drink or religion. Drink was undoubtedly a terrible scourge and the cause of much distress and poverty, and was therefore much feared and preached against. Although the Scriptures said 'strong drink is raging', it also said 'be fruitful and multiply', thus, if drink was out sex was in. Large families were the result, any number from 15 to 20 children being quite normal, which did not help the situation. The Hillarys with only six children were quite modest, and showed a degree of understanding not general in their day. They were to have another child 'Ethel', but she did not arrive until after their return to England and thus does not figure in the diary. At the moment, however, they are still aboard ship, but the children are to cause them anxiety before New Zealand is reached.

Friday 2nd January. (Thirtysixth day) 219 miles. 'Nothing very remarkable excepting the heat which is excessive. Although over the line by 1271 miles yet on account of it being winter at home and mid-summer in the antipodes, we are just now about directly under the sun's rays at noonday, and almost melting away.'

Saturday 3rd January. (Thirtyseventh day) 206 miles. 'Lost the most unfaithful companion I ever had, for he only stood by me in the sunshine, and in the dark and cloudy day was never to be seen. However, although my shadow is gone because I am directly under the sun, I suppose I shall have a new one from the other side in a few days. We expect tonight to be out of the Tropic of Capricorn.'

Sunday 4th January. (Thirtyeighth day) 189 miles. 'Calling the muster roll, and reading a dry service by doctor and Captain, giving out dinner, water, bread, milk, etc. and this holy day made for man the brightest of the seven, which was always to me such a delight at home, gives one no pleasure, but pain to see it so spent. Shut out from the services of the Sanctuary I envy those "Happy birds that sing and fly round Thy altars, Oh Most High". When the voyage is ended my greatest joy will be to appear before God in Zion.'

Monday 5th January. (Thirtyninth day) 198 miles. 'Heat abating. Are going spendidly. Allowance of lime juice and extra water discontinued. Edith has taken measles.'

Tuesday 6th January. (Fortieth day) 221 miles. 'Another trial, Edith and Albert both down in the measles and by doctor's orders we are to go with them into the Hospital on deck. As there are other cases on board it is feared we shall on arrival be ordered into quarantine, which must be unless the passengers have been free from all infection for one lunar month. We are going with a good wind, and the hope of the officials that we shall yet make a quick voyage, seems to be reviving. We expect to reach the latitude of the Cape of Good Hope tomorrow. Thought much of my class, and a little after 4 o'clock I joined them in spirit, it being 7.30 with them.'

We see how good can come out of misfortune, in that on account of illness among the children, our travellers are transferred to a cabin on deck. The doctor was to prove most kind to them throughout the rest of the voyage. It must have been a great improvement to have the privacy of a deck cabin after the communal quarters below, and they were to have what virtually amounted to first-class accommodation from now on.

Wednesday 7th January. (Fortyfirst day) 215 miles. 'Fred took measles in the night but they are all favourably held, and we hope with good nursing may soon recover. Willie and John Tom are, of course, in the single men's apartments out of the way. We prefer the Hospital on the main deck to the berths. Saw several porpoises, and a ship passed us at noon. Mamma was delighted because, with the glass, she could see people on the poop. About 3 pm, the "Famenoth" a fine ship of Shaw Savill & Company, bound from Auckland to London passed close by us, there was much waving of handkerchiefs and shouting on each side. It is quite remarkable, we had both been out 41 days, and met halfway. We wondered to see so many passengers returning on this ship, if N.Z. is so prosperous, and England so dull, why return?'

We read here about the 'Famenoth' returning from Auckland. This is most unusual for a sailing ship to be returning in this direction, the usual method being to continue eastwards across the Pacific Ocean and round the much dreaded Cape Horn into the South Atlantic and home. It was to be three years later before Shaw Savill & Company ventured into steam, so this vessel must have been a sailer; steamers of course could return using the Suez Canal. Be that as it may, John Hillary was quick to note the number of people returning, and the first seeds of doubt were here sown. Little did he realise at this time what was to await him on his arrival.

It is interesting to read in the next entry of Mother's daily bottle of stout, so if John Hillary was teetotal 'Mamma' was obviously not. As stated previously, the diarist had not always been a non-drinker and the writer can remember his Grandmother telling him how this came about. It would appear that in their early married life it was necessary for John Hillary to visit many of the local farms on business. While there it was customary for a bottle to be opened and a drink or two consumed, thus John Hillary sometimes used to arrive home, if not drunk at least decidedly 'merry'. This caused Mrs. H. considerable anxiety, which was noted by her husband, who having insisted upon an explanation, was informed of the reason. His answer was simply to stop drinking from that moment and henceforth he became a rabid T.T. It is possible that it was from then that he turned to religion, because it is hardly likely at that time that a religious person would touch drink, the two just did not mix. Certainly, if the church might condone some drinking, Chapel certainly did not, and as we know John Hillary was a non-conformist.

Thursday 8th January. (Fortysecond day) 65 miles. 'Children going on all right, and we are very comfortable in the Hospital, as well off as cabin passengers, having the room to ourselves. Dr. Russell visits us about four times daily, and supplys us with chicken soup, arrowroot, sago, and anything the children can eat, also a bottle of stout daily for mother, so that her vigils may not weary her out. We are rounding the Cape and the weather is very enjoyable, having left the long-remembered heat of the tropics behind. Several albatrosses flying around us, and passed through a shoal of sturgeons, the shouting and laughing at their antics in the water being deafening.'

Friday 9th January. (Fortythird day) 113 miles. 'Seven alabtrosses surrounded us this morning, and after dinner, with the aid of a baited hook, one was caught. It is a pretty bird about 20 lbs weight, its' wings stretched out measuring from tip to tip 9 feet 4 ins. Children improving but another case has broken out on the ship. Seven weeks today we *left home*'.

Saturday 10 January. (Fortyfourth day) 82 miles. 'Have heard much about the solemnity of a burial at sea but today have witnessed one. The little daughter of J. Smith of North Allerton, aged two years, died of measles at 5 am and at 11.30 am her body was committed to the deep, until, at the fiat of Him who is the Resurrection and the Life, the greedy sea shall yield her dead. A vessel bound from London to Adelaide named "Pakwan" passed us afternoon, and our first mate went over to her in a boat, with letters to send home from the Cape. This caused a great stir.'

Sunday 11th January. (Fortyfifth day) 71 miles. 'The Sabbath is to me the most wearisome day of the week, inasmuch as it forcibly reminds one of those blessed Christian privileges I enjoyed at home, but am now deprived of. Reading "Service", giving out beef, water, milk and bread, and the day with a painful retrospect is gone. Children are doing well.'

Monday 12th January. (Fortysixth day) 104 miles. 'Weekly rations served out. Some fresh cases of sickness among the children, but ours are convalescent. Dr. Russell is most assiduous and tender in his attentions to them. He has had to lance a large sea lump on Fred's head which has discharged a quantity of matter. Most people on board have these or other eruptions caused by the heat of the tropics.'

Tuesday 13th January. (Fortyseventh day) 100 miles. 'Was

WESTLAND

out at 5.30 am and saw a whale blowing up. Large flocks of albatrosses, mollyhawks, Capehens, Cape pigeons, and Mother Carey's chickens flying round us. Had a good wind all day and tonight the sea is running high and the "Westland" is dashing along at a great pace.'

Wednesday 14th January. (Fortyeighth day) 208 miles. 'A cool day and high sea. Glass standing at 59 in berths. Saw a lot of mule porpoises in front of the ship this morning which swam about a mile with us. They are pretty fish with brown backs and white bellies, about 28 lbs weight and shaped like a mackerel. They who go down to the sea in ships behold the works of the Lord and His wonders in the deep.'

Thursday 15th January. (Fortyninth day) 187 miles. Several albatrosses and mollyhawks about us. Sailors busy tidying all up for making the ship respectable before she reaches Lyttleton Harbour, and fastening down spare spars and boats as though there were indications of a storm and a shaking. They say we will not have any more calms and may run 350 miles a day yet, as this is the place for wind.'

Friday 16th January. (Fiftieth day) 207 miles. 'Eight weeks today we left home, would that we have another home. We do not forget pay Friday, and talk of what people will be doing at Tow Law. Mamma says many of them in business will be mourning over short payments, increasing balances, pressing liabilities etc., and trying hard, like the dog after his tail, to make ends meet.'

Here we have the most likely explanation of John Hillary's reasons for emigrating, and we learn that although he was a tradesman, running a business was not without its troubles. There is mention of 'short payments', 'increasing balances', and finally 'pressing liabilities'. We must bear in mind that most of the customers were mining folk and the miner was only paid for the coal he produced. Thus, if the seam he was working contained more stone than coal the collier got 'short pay' at the end of the week. The shopkeeper was expected to help out until conditions improved, which he did, but it made business very difficult and not likely to produce large profits.

Saturday 17th January. (Fiftyfirst day) 191 miles. 'Cold weather. Herbert poorly and apparently beginning with measles. Flour and raisins given out for Sunday's dumplings. Have now sailed over 7,000 miles and are still rounding the Cape of Good Hope, but going wide of it. Sailors are lashing everything moveable on deck and we think this ominous of squalls.'

Sunday 18th January. (Fiftysecond day) 221 miles. 'Very high sea. Ship rolling very much. Had this been the first week we should all have been ill today. At noon our time was on a par with Greenwich. Roll called, but no service because of the rough weather. I had a severe attack of spasms about 2 am and Mamma had to send the watchman aft to the doctor, who sent me a dose of strong mint. Am better today, but sore. Water bottles, flour tubs etc. have all to be lashed and tin plates, dishes etc. are chasing each other about the floor. She pitches fearfully.'

Monday 19th January. (Fiftythird day) 245 miles. 'Water and milk at 6.30 am. Children's meat and soup at seven. To cook house to toast bread and get coffee and porridge for breakfast at eight. Sweeping and scouring under berths at 9 am. Going to store for weekly supply of sugar, coffee, tea, butter, salt, pepper, and mustard during forenoon. Pea soup, boiled salt beef and carrot for dinner. Bread and butter or tinned meat and rice to tea at 5. Had great difficulty in getting our food as the ship is rolling so much, several fell on deck and our plates and food frequently fly off the form during meals. Friends at home would be terrified, but we old sailors seem to think nothing of it as we sit with the door open, watching the ship going down on one side almost beneath the surging waves, then rising right above them until we have to hold on by anything we can catch to keep on deck. Time, 25 minutes before London.'

The reference to 'tinned meat' is interesting, the writer was unaware that any canning was done so early in the eighties. We can only assume this must have been that same 'bully beef' that helped to win the 1914/18 war. The sailors had been right to get everything moveable lashed down, they obviously knew what to expect. From now onwards long daily runs are registered.

Tuesday 20th January. (Fiftyfourth day) 203 miles. 'After a night of rocking on account of a stern wind we have got the wind on the quarter today, and are going smartly but steadily, a side wind is always best. Herbert continues very poorly indeed.'

Wednesday 21st January. (Fiftyfifth day) 252 miles. 'Weather cool and bracing. Having no fires to warm us we have to pace the deck to keep up natural heat. Going fast. Our baby, Herbert, is very ill and in addition to the measles has got inflammation of the chest. Sickness is bad at home, but how much worse at sea, without a friend to sympathise with you, or a fire to warm you.'

Thursday 22nd January. (Fiftysixth day) 267 miles. 'Eight weeks today since we set sail. Another stowaway appeared this morning, I suppose he is a big Irish boy (McGrath). Herbert is a trifle better but still in great danger. With a fog and a south wind, the weather is cold and comfortless, but landsmen hardly know what those terms mean here, for nothing wet at sea seems to dry, but retains a clammy dampness which is most unpleasant to feel.'

Friday 23rd January. (Fiftyseventh day) 165 miles. 'Baby about as yesterday. Storm expected. Caught by a line and hook a fine albatross, measuring 10 ft. from tip to tip of wings, and 5 ft. from bill to tail. Nine weeks today we left our dear friends and home. Oh, the charm of that word "home", I never felt its sweetness or valued its comforts until now.'

It is surprising to read of the cold weather. They were just below the latitude of Cape Town, and further away from the Antarctic than we are from the Polar regions. But it must be remembered the South Pole is a land mass, and produces by far the largest icebergs which travel greater distances before melting, and chill the sea over a wider area. Furthermore the wind was southerly, blowing from the Antarctic Continent, which must have made conditions in an unheated ship very miserable. This together with the storms, the sickness of Baby Herbert, and the continual dampness aboard, must have made 'Home' seem a very pleasant place indeed.

Saturday, 24th January. (Fiftyeighth day) 207 miles. 'The expected storm came this morning and raged all day furiously. Mrs. H. and children all kept their beds, and I only ventured out when obliged. Several people got bad falls on deck, among whom was Isaac Whiting, whose feet shot out like greased lightning, and he landed in the scooper (scupper?) under the spars with such force the sailors sarcastically asked if he was trying to knock the bulwarks out. A sea caught several of the single women and almost drowned them, they had to got to bed until their clothes were dried. Many got bad bruises from being dashed down, and Mr. Phillips, the first Mate, was sorely hurt. The carpenter's bench was smashed, and our Willie fell and spilt his porridge. Tedious as the voyage has become to us, we should prefer being rather longer on the ship than having a recurrence of this day's tossing. Baby is very little better.'

Sunday 25th January. (Fiftyninth day) 276 miles. 'The storm abated somewhat about noon, but in the morning it was very dangerous moving about deck. No roll call on account of the stormy weather. The thoughts of home comforts made me very sick of sea life, oh, that this voyage was ended, and its godless associations. We have much wickedness, but no prayers, no Christian fellowship, no Sanctuary. The faces, voices, forms, times and unction of the old Chapel all no longer to cheer me, and the people, houses, fields, and roads recur to my memory now, with a vividness no pen can describe. However, my confidence in the wisdom and goodness of that Providence who has guided me my life long and directed my way here, is as firm as ever it was. I suppose, when we land and I am employed, my mind will rest again.'

Monday 26th January. (Sixtieth day) 273 miles. 'Have still a strong wind and dashing along swiftly. Captain says he thinks at this rate we shall land in eighteen days. The weather is very cold, and having no fires to sit aside, we feel it keenly. Herbert is no better.'

Tuesday 27th January. (Sixtyfirst day) 232 miles. 'The first Mate is able to resume his duties again after his fall. Baby is still in great danger, not having strength to expectorate the phlegm caused by the inflammation in his lungs. A sea voyage may be beneficial if short, but this one is too long, and the climatic changes are exceedingly trying to adults, but too severe by far for little children.'

Wednesday, 28th January. (Sixtysecond day) 225 miles. 'Scores of birds flying round the ship. Weather very cold and dull. Baby worse. I must here correct a mistaken notion we had, and our friends will still have, that the sea looks flat and you can see as far as the eye will carry. Every way you look the sea appears round, the ship always seems to be in a hollow and you think, looking ahead, you have only a hill to go over and you will get faster away, but this is always the same. The ocean meets the sky and the masts of a coming ship look like small sticks rising out of the sea.'

Thursday 29th January. (Sixtythird day) 291 miles. 'Weather cloudy and foggy. Caught another albatross 9 ft. 9 inches from tip to tip of wings. Have been sailing 9 weeks and done 10,036 miles. Our little son is no better, and the congestion of the lungs having been so severe his recovery is very doubtful.'

Friday 30th January. (Sixtyfourth day) 100 miles. 'Dr. Russell has given Herbert up this morning, and though this news is distressing it is not unexpected, for I saw a few days ago "that death had marked him out an offering for the tomb". When friends at home read this they will know what my feelings are today, far away upon the pathless sea, friendless and homeless. Oh, Lord, give me Abraham's faith and obedience. Caught another albatross this evening 10 feet from tip to tip of wings. Witnessed this evening the most gorgeous eastern sunset we have yet seen, but to describe its grandeur I am quite unable.'

The diarist is evidently going through a very trying period. No sight of land, and he mentions in a further entry, five weeks without seeing even another ship. But for the somewhat surprising appearance of the 'Famenoth' on Jan. 7 the interval would have been even longer. The cold and the severe illness of Baby Herbert did not help, together with the clammy dampness of all clothing etc. which any yachtsman knows only too well. No polythene bags then available to keep things dry. As John Hillary says, it was bad enough for the adults but for the children with only the confines of the ship to roam about in, it must have been terribly boring. Coupled with this, was the complete isolation and total lack of any communication with the outside world. For weeks or months on end travellers by sea had no knowledge whatever of what was happening in the world around them, and until their ship arrived at some port their whereabouts were quite unknown. Thus, very many ships and their crews just disappeared, lost without trace. It is difficult to convey to the modern reader the utter loneliness of the sea in those days. Even John Hillary was quite unaware that his Mother, mentioned at the beginning of the diary, was by this time dead and buried – she died on December 11th, less than one month after the diarist said goodbye to her at Darlington on November 21st. He was not to learn of her death until he arrived in New Zealand. Surely such travellers understood the full meaning of the words 'the lonely sea and the sky', because these had been their constant companions for many weeks.

Saturday 31st January. (Sixtyfifth day) 57 miles. 'A fine day but little wind. A whale and many porpoises seen and a Mollyhawk caught. Herbert is wasting for want of support and cannot take it.'

Sunday 1st February. (Sixtysixth day) 167 miles. 'Captain said to us at roll call this morning "Three weeks this morning you will be going to church in New Zealand". Won't that be a joy if true? At muster Captain read out some charges against one of the young men passengers named Thomas Robinson of being drunk and with some of the sailors breaking into the ship's stores and stealing therefrom spirits etc. They are to be prosecuted on arrival in port. Baby Herbert is still sinking.

Monday 2nd February. (Sixtyseventh day) 226 miles. 'Have been sitting up all night with our dear baby as the pressages of death are upon him. He still lingers however, but how soon we shall have to give him to the sharks we know not. I feel this affliction most keenly and have weakened myself by grief. "He who has most of heart knows most of sorrow".

Tuesday 3rd February. (Sixtyeighth day) 198 miles. 'Herbert is a little easier but we fear whether the improvement will be permanent. More birds caught and some of the passengers are busy skinning them the breasts for muffs, bones for burnishing leather and pipe stems and the skin of the feet for tobacco pouches. John Payne's eldest girl very ill, I fear fatally so.'

It is rather surprising to read several accounts of the capture and killing of an Albatross. For many years it has been considered that to sailors the Albatross was a bird of ill omen and for that reason sacrosant and not to be killed. Many stories have been told of supposed disasters to vessels as the result of the killing of an Albatross and we have the well known poem of the Ancient Mariner. It must be admitted in that instance the bird was shot. It seems the passengers and crew of the 'Westland' had scant regard for these birds, but perhaps like the fox the Albatross must not be shot. The mention of 'Muffs' may puzzle the younger lady readers, these were worn by women in those days to keep the hands warm in winter.

Wednesday 4th February. (Sixtyninth day) 178 miles. 'Strange to say Herbert is a little brighter and beginning to take a little support. Weather very cold but having a good wind our ship is dashing along at a rare speed.'

Thursday 5th February. (Seventieth day) 272 miles. 'Baby still improving. It is ten weeks since we set sail and to all appearances within a fortnight we shall be in harbour and thence to quarantine which seems now to be a certainty for us. However, we shall be on land and have a change of diet which will be of great benefit. We need some vegetable food our blood is heated and skin itching.'

Friday 6th February. (Seventyfirst day) 256 miles. 'A rough sea and stormy day, but we are going at a fine speed. Baby much better, and to all appearances he is to escape the sharks and see the goodly land.'

Saturday 7th February. (Seventysecond day) 258 miles. 'Dr. Russell says there is a marked improvement in Herbert, who is beginning to eat well. The kindness and attentions of Dr. Russell are beyond all praise, and with chicken broth, medicine, and wine would have cost us pounds in England. Another birth during the night, a "gal" (Robinson).'

Sunday 8th February. (Seventythird day) 255 miles. 'Fine day, Sailing well. Herbert progressing. Our time is now eight hours before London, so that when our friends at home were getting breakfast we were having tea. This we hope will be the last Sunday but one on board. At Dr's request I preached between decks tonight to an attentive audience. Took the parable of the "Ten Virgins", had good liberty and a blessed unction, Lord help me to live a useful and powerful life. Heard of one rather queer woman on board, making her children say prayers before going to bed after the service.'

Baby Herbert is progressing and this must have been a great relief to our travellers and good fortune to the writer for Baby Herbert was destined to become my father some 24 years later. He lived to be 70 years old and died in Queen Elizabeth's Hospital, Birmingham, and of what? Congestion of the lungs. So I lost an excellent father from the same complaint he had suffered from all those years ago when perhaps some weakness had been retained.

Monday 9th February. (Seventyfourth day) 275 miles. 'Going well. Herbert rapidly recovering. Weekly supplies of provisions given out, and no bills to pay nor any losses to mourn. Have plenty to eat, and more than we can use of some things, but the fare becomes so monotonous that the stomach almost refuses it.'

Tuesday 10th February. (Seventyfifth day) 267 miles. 'We

expect, if we keep this wind for another week, to land. Are now going along the Australian coast, but too far off to see it.'

Wednesday 11th February. (Seventysixth day) 156 miles. 'Wind eased about 1.am. and we are now going slowly. The cold has passed away, and we are having fine weather, as we near the land of the Southern Cross.'

Thursday 12th February. (Seventyseventh day) 151 miles. 'A second child of Mr. Tarlings died about 9.am, of dropsy after measles, and at 11 o'clock this morning we committed his body to the gaping waves. Eleven weeks today we set sail, and in another week we hope to cast anchor in Lyttleton harbour. Sailors are as busy as the "Devil in a whirlwind" making all look spliff. Herbert is almost well again, his recovery having been wonderfully rapid.'

The Tarlings were most unlucky to lose two children on the voyage, both as a result of the after effects of measles. This disease was a scourge last century and early this, but owing to increased medical knowledge and vaccination it is by no means so serious as it then was. Strange to relate the next day was Baby Herbert's first birthday but the diarist fails to mention this.

Friday 13th February. (Seventyeighth day) 215 miles. 'Twelve weeks today we left home. Excepting being far away and on the sea we know nothing to trouble us, our income is nothing but our outlay and losses are no more, we have none of those bad pays which used to destroy our peace of mind, and unfit us for life's duties. And the "begaring travellers" don't come here.'

Saturday 14th February. (Seventyninth day) 159 miles. 'Postman did not bring us any Valentines this morning. Am far away from Hedley Hill today. Three Albatrosses and five mollyhawks caught today. Are on the coast of Tasmania but not able to see it. What strange Saturday nights these are, indeed as there is nothing to make any difference in this monotonous life all days are wearily alike.'

Sunday 15th February. (Eightieth day) 258 miles. 'Going well with a good wind. Payne's eldest girl is sinking. I preached this evening from the last text I used at Tow Law "Wherewithal shall a young man cleanse his way". People listened attentively and I hope good was done. Am now going to my little narrow bed, it is just gone eleven and our friends at home will only have finished dinner it being 1.pm, with them.'

Monday 16th February. (Eightyfirst day) 293 miles. 'Are all busy scrubbing and washing our bunks out for landing. I have been down between decks washing ours out, although it has been standing vacant during the six weeks we have occupied the snug little cabbin on the main deck.'

Tuesday 17th February. (Eightysecond day) 258 miles. 'Sighted a vessel ahead this morning and not having seen one for five weeks it caused some excitement. No ships return to England this way but keep still going on East and go round the other side of the globe, this would seem strange to landsmen. At about 6.30 in the morning our time my class will be meeting at 7.30 in the evening at Tow Law, our time being now 11 hours before theirs. What a pleasure it would be to meet them now.'

Wednesday 18th February. (Eightythird day) 173 miles. 'John Payne having been keeping vigils over his two children all night, who are dangerously ill, called me up before 5.am, to see those black rocks or coral islands called "The Snares" in longitude 166, which we were passing. They look like the walls of an old castle in height and length. At 4.pm, we sighted the end of South Island or Otago coast round which we go to Lyttelton. Have anchors ready to cast and expect soon to be in harbour. Tonight the light from Port Chalmers shines brightly.'

Nearly eight weeks have elapsed since any mention of land being sighted and five weeks without even seeing a ship. In fact although this was the 18th February they had not seen land since the previous year, on 29th December. It seems incredible in these days that this could happen and under these conditions. The 'Westland' was far removed from the luxury liner of today and by comparison very small indeed. There were no facilities for any form of amusement and with the exception of the few concerts on deck (and none of these for a long time), no entertainment of any sort. No wonder the passengers were happy to catch a few sea birds and skin them, and what pastimes the children had is not mentioned. We can imagine with what longing John Hillary looked forward to the end of the voyage and being an active man, getting into harness again. He was not at this moment to know that many months would pass before he would be at work again and that would be back in Old England.

How fortunate it is sometimes that we are not permitted to know the future and although there are times one feels this is a great drawback it is, on the whole, probably for the better. It was certainly better for the diarist to be ignorant at this time. Having endured almost three months at sea with all its vicissitudes, hopes must now have been running high. It was unfortunate they would have to go into quarantine but at least they would be on land and not subject to the continual motion of the ship.

They had virtually reached New Zealand but were unfortunately, from their point of view, approaching it from the wrong side. To reach Lyttleton it was necessary to turn South and sail round the coast of Otago, the southern end of South Island, through the Foveaux Strait, between Stewart Island and the mainland, before sailing North. Thence half way up the other side of South Island to Banks Peninsular; behind this lies Lyttleton, the port for Christchurch which was to be their final destination. Incidentally in part of South Island is the province of Westland from which the ship was named.

Thursday 19th February. (Eightyfourth day) 202 miles. 'We are only 150 miles from port but the wind having ceased are almost standing. Had raisin dumpling and sauce, preserved meat, carrots and bread for dinner and Dr. gave half a bottle of porter and a quarter of sherry to each family. The day is beautifully sunny and warm, whales blowing up near us and numerous birds off the coast flying around us. Tonight a rat came in at the cabin door and terrified Edith and Fred until we got it caught and killed.'

Friday 20th February. (Eightyfifth day) 100 miles. 'Are almost becalmed on the coast such are the uncertainties of

NEW ZEALAND

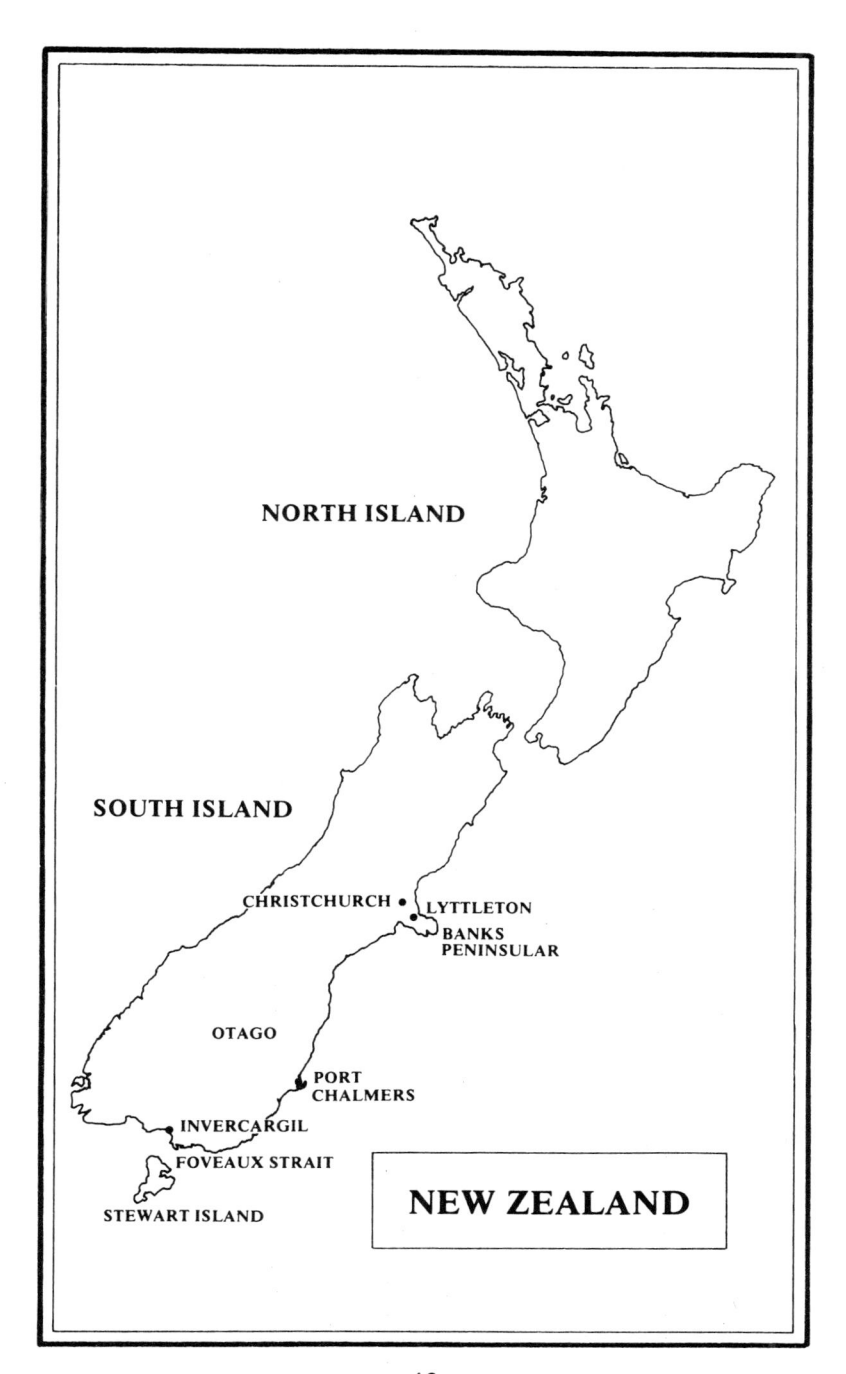

- NORTH ISLAND
- SOUTH ISLAND
- CHRISTCHURCH
- LYTTLETON
- BANKS PENINSULAR
- OTAGO
- PORT CHALMERS
- INVERCARGIL
- FOVEAUX STRAIT
- STEWART ISLAND

sailing ships. A fair wind would easily have put us into harbour this afternoon. Sails are altered every few minutes and we are sailing backwards and forwards but not able to round Banks Peninsular, from whence a revolving light shines brightly tonight. Seaweed in great quantities and land birds attract our attention, also a small red fish like shrimps in size called sea spiders, in such quantities as to make the water in some places appear as red as blood.'

Saturday 21st February. (Eightysixth day) 50 miles. 'After drifting about several hours near the shore this morning with a foul wind we hailed a pretty steamer bound from Timaru to Lyttleton by which we asked to be reported. The Captain treated us kindly and promised to report us and the cook stepped to the door of the galley and smilingly held up a leg of mutton before our longing eyes. Afternoon a steam tug named after the harbour came and towed us in. By the mercy of God we are anchored in the splendid harbour of Lyttleton. We had not been anchored many minutes before a boat came alongside us and put an abundance of provisions on board, the flesh including a whole carcass, the vegetables, bread, milk, eggs, etc. being all fresh and good. That we regarded them as dainties I need hardly say. My diary will show my varied experiences and feelings during the voyage, but all my hopes of the beauties of the place and the fineness of the climate are fully realized, and the discomforts of the voyage seem already to be disappearing. But that we are ordered into quarantine is another trial, however, we hope it won't be long before we have our liberty again.'

Sunday 22nd February. 'Were this morning taken off the "Westland" and landed at the Quarantine Station on Ripa Island which is almost opposite Lyttleton about 3 miles across the bay, and 3 acres in extent. The buildings, which are neat and clean, are all wooden, painted and covered with corrugated iron. We can fish, bathe, and enjoy ourselves.'

And that was the last the diarist and his family were to see of the 'Noble Westland' that had been their home for three months, and had carried them safely to their land of promise. We shall read what became of the Hillarys, but of the ship, what was to become of her? The 'Westland' I have reason to believe, sailed under the house flag of Shaw Savill until 1906 when she was sold to C. Hannevig of Norway. She was, however, not destined to sail for long under her new owners because in 1909, having left Barbados in the West Indies, she ran into such bad weather she had to put into Kingston, Jamaica, disabled, there she was condemned and broken up. Thus ended a fine ship, after many splendid voyages, and by the long arm of coincidence John Tom went to live at Kingston in the 1920s. It would be interesting to know whether he ever discovered the fate of the 'Westland', but this we shall never know, for he, like the ship, has gone on his last voyage.

I feel I cannot conclude the account of the outward voyage without paying a special tribute to one man, Doctor Russell. Throughout John Hillary's diary of this voyage one name runs like a shining light and to this one man so much was owed, and not realised, by the passengers on the 'Westland'.

Lucky indeed were they to have been chosen to travel on such a fine vessel, but how different might have been the voyage without Dr. Russell and how many of them would have reached New Zealand? We shall read in the next entry what happened to the travellers on the second ship, the 'Earl Granville' for by the time she reached Lyttleton 'About 100 passengers had died beside the doctor, and the remainder were dying like rotten sheep and filthy with vermin.' Such could well have been the case on the 'Westland' but for Dr. Russell's constant attention and quick realisation of the situation when lice first appeared. It is true that deaths did occur, but considering the length of the voyage and the medical knowledge and facilities which Dr. Russell then had at his disposal, these deaths would appear to be only proportionate to the natural wastage normally occurring in the same number of people and in the same period of time on land. The death rate among young people was far higher then than in modern times, certainly what deaths took place were not from lack of attention on Dr. Russell's part.

When Baby Herbert was ill we read of the doctor's four visits per day and later of the wine and soup etc. which John Hillary admits 'would have cost pounds in England'. We also read of the doctors 'many kindnesses' and we imagine this does not just relate to the Hillary family. The writer must also express his own gratitude to the doctor as without his care and attention to Baby Herbert I would not have been alive today.

Finally, there is the skipper, Captain Wood, about whom we read very little. What we do read, however, is never to his discredit, apart from the diarist's reference to swearing and leading the dance. This in all probability did not make him any worse than average, and the diarist was admittedly somewhat sanctimonious. Captain Wood seems to have been a good skipper and brought the 'Westland' safely into port with no troubles of any sort. He was not often captain of the 'Westland', and had previously only done one out and home voyage in her, and the return journey on this occasion was to be his last in this ship.

Friday 12th March 1880. 'Were taken off Ripa Island by the little steamer and via Lyttleton, by train, arrived at Christchurch in the evening. We lodged the first night at Mother Bleigh's Restaurant where we found a good cup of tea and the soft beds very acceptable. Next morning we set up house in New Street, where we had to pay 12/- per week in advance for a four roomed wooden house with cooking range so useless we could not cook our food, and after remaining here three weeks we removed to King Street, Sandridge, into a better house at the same rental. Here we remained until the six months of our colonial life were ended, and we returned home to England. In finishing the diary of our outward voyage let me again refer to the den of disease, the Government Depot at Plymouth, where the seed of the fatal disease on the two ships was doubtless sown. The bad arrangements and crowded state of that wretched place arose from the fact that the officials admit some of the filthiest specimens of the human race, whose dirty persons must engender disease, and in our case the emigrants for both the 'Westland' and the 'Earl Granville' were brought there at the same time and crowded together like a flock of sheep. Besides the sickness and deaths on our ship, the New Zealand newspapers reported that when the 'Earl Granville', which left Plymouth two days after us, arrived, about 100 passengers had died, beside the doctor, the remainder were in quarantine, and they were dying like rotten sheep, and filthy with vermin.'

The Hillary family: Standing, left to right – Fred, Albert, Herbert. Seated, left to right – Willie, Edith, John Hillary, Mamma, Ethel, John Tom.

View across the Pennines from Tow Law

the right & oumt on the are, as far as the eye can see, nothing but rock sand & barrenness everywhere, however inland are the beauties of all countries. Suez Canal is 93 miles long, is cut through the land of Goshen, & varies in width from 50 yards to five or 6 miles, where it goes through two lakes. It is worked by telegraphic communication, & sidings are provided at intervals for Steamers to wait in passing. In the narrow places great care is needed, and we only went about 4 miles per hour, but in the Lakes about 10 miles. On the banks on either side small native hamlets are springing up, with their flat roofed sand or concrete built houses of one story, some of which have small gardens & a few trees growing in them. Women are standing a the doors, at least such I took them to be, but their dress makes the sexes difficult to distinguish, children playing round, dogs lounging & goats grazing on the scanty poor herbage, on which only goats, donkeys, & camels can subsist. One of these houses attracted attention particularly,

A page from John Hillary's diary

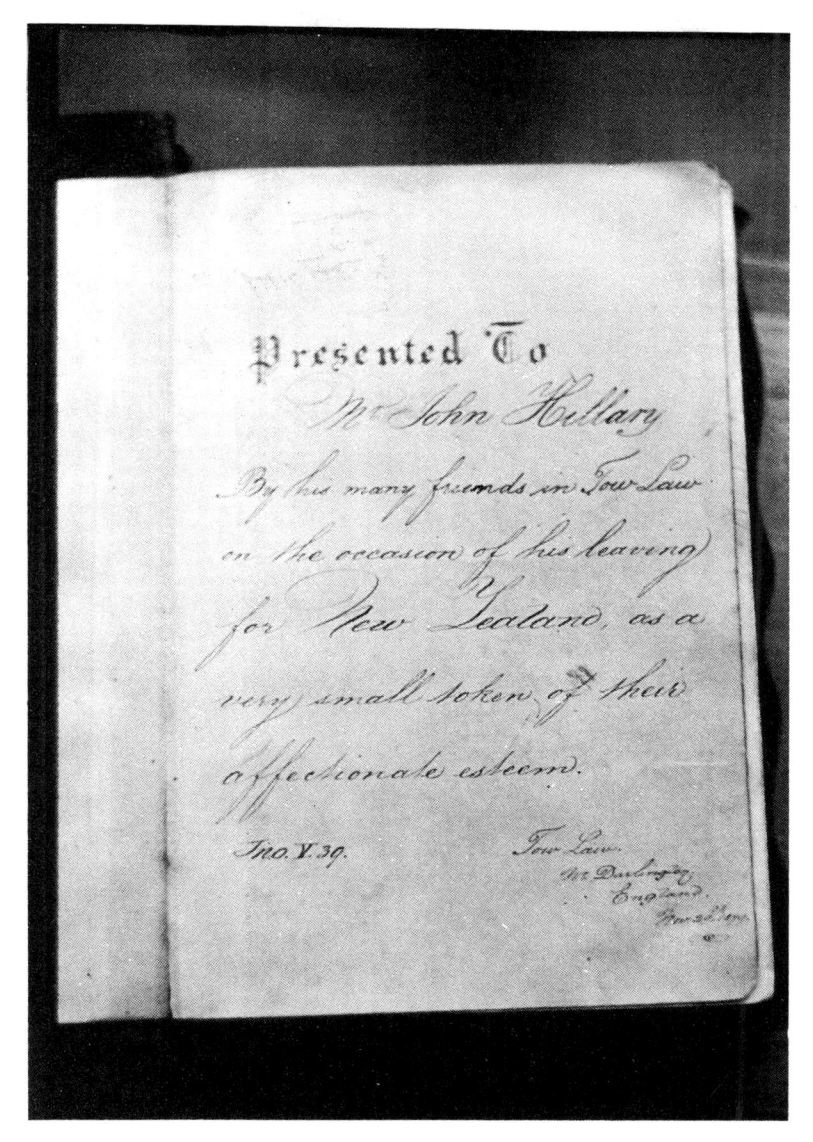

Dedication page of the Bible given to John Hillary by his Tuesday Bible Class

Dans Castle, Tow Law

Milk delivery, Tow Law

New Zealand

Before reading the diarist's account of his experiences in New Zealand and the conditions he found there it is necessary for the reader to understand fully the value of the pound sterling and its effect on wages and prices at that time. The spending power of the pound was then some twenty times greater than it is today, and as we shall see John Hillary mentions people in England earning £1 or £2 per week before emigrating. This may seem unbelievably small wages today, but quite the reverse was the case in the 1800s. £1 to £2 per week was quite high and lower paid workers at that time were paid in shillings per week and many did not even approach £1 weekly. The old penny would buy goods to the value of nearly 10 pence today. Thus the old half-penny and farthing were coins of value and in frequent use. The writer, who was not born until this century, can well remember being able to buy sweets for one farthing and as a small boy was given one old penny per week as pocket or spending money.

   It was during and after the 1914-1918 war that money really began to lose its value when coins were replaced by paper money. Before that time coins contained enough metal, copper, silver and gold to cover their value anywhere in the world. We can see therefore that when the diarist mentions men leaving jobs of around £2 to emigrate to New Zealand these men had left highly paid work or had held good positions here in England. In one instance mention is made of a man losing £350 – this would amount to some £7000 today.

CHRISTCHURCH 'A city of 24,000 people standing on the sides of the serpentine river Avon which is crossed by about 20 bridges and on the banks of which the stately Poplar and Weeping Willow grow so luxuriantly as often to meet at the top and form an arch over the river. Like the new Jerusalem the city lieth foursquare, its streets, which are 50 to 70 yards wide, run parallel from east to west and north to south crossing each other at right angles and are a mile in length from belt to belt of the city proper. This however only represents about one third of its extent. The streets have grown so far over the town belt and it is intended soon to extend the belt to two miles, but even when the streets grow to five miles the same order will be maintained.

'The houses which, excepting for business places in the centre of the city many of which are of brick or concrete, are nearly all built of wood and stand detached upon quarter, half, or acre sections of land. They are very pretty many having a good deal of taste displayed in their design, are nicely painted, with verandahs in front on which stand a couple of chairs, and a grass plot or flower garden in front. Some of them have fountains playing the year round, for perhaps Christchurch is the best watered city in the world. It is often said it stands upon a latent reservoir and it is a remarkable fact that you have only to tap the rock and the water gushes out.

'Suppose you build a house, you select a place in your garden for your well, then employ a professional artesian well sinker. He puts a pipe plugged at one end with about one inch bore upon the spot, puts a rod up the inside and a heavy weight with a hole up the middle to fit the rod upon the pipe. He then fixes up three legs and a pulley which he puts ropes across and pulls the weight up and drops it upon the pipe until it is driven to the proper stratum when he drives out the plug and the pure water flows up with great force. A bend-pipe is put on the end and a box placed beneath, the outflow being turned through the garden into the open channel in the street so that in the heat of summer the pedestrian has a cooling stream of water flowing by his feet. The water is left running and never dries up. Two or three days before washing the wife takes her dirty linen in a coarse bag and lays it into the box, where it steeps and bleaches as white as snow.'

THE PEOPLE. 'The Maories are tall, robust, and not treacherous like most aboriginal tribes. The Europeans are clever, sharp, shrewd, respectful but very selfish people. He who goes out expecting to teach them anything will be mistaken. Even children, well educated and quick. Sharp but pretty talkers, accent Yankee and Cockney.'

RELIGION 'In a declining state. The people seem so engrossed by this world their energies are all used up. Although they have fine churches and contribute freely to the cause, they do not care for much experimental preaching.'

COLONIAL PHRASES
'Shout for all round.
Chuck.
Go for him.
Good on you.
Cooie.
Gassy. (too much gas)

Clear out.
Vault.
Up a tree.
He done to me.
Staunch horse.
A terror.

Get the smell of lime juice and pea soup off you.'

OPINION OF NEW ZEALAND 'Climate, all that it was represented and quite equal to our expectations. More equable than that of England and so much finer that winter is as good as an indifferent English summer. The sky is so clear and the atmosphere so thin that the sun, moon and stars seem to shine far brighter and distance is so difficult to estimate that mountains and objects 50 miles away don't appear to be over 5, and photographs taken here are far clearer than those taken at home. Many garden flowers remain in bloom the year round and the trees don't cast their faded leaves as at home. On the shortest day of the year we have daylight from 7 am to 5 pm. Twilight short. Even in mid-winter the days are generally sunny, sometimes very warm so that a man cannot work or walk freely with his coat on, but at sundown he must put an extra one on. For although the nights are not as cold as English winter nights, the heat of the day thins the blood so much that the nights are in Colonial phraseology a "Terror for cold". The heat of the summer is very little more than at home but even then so cool are the nights sleepers can always bear the blankets upon them. The extremes between day and night are far greater than in England. Walking along the foot of the hills and by the side of the Heathcote river on July 18th, corresponding to January in England I sat down on the river's bank and almost wept aloud because I could not make my way in such a fine country, and to all appearances would be obliged to leave it. The river as clear as crystal is fed by artesian springs bubbling up in its bed and springs flowing out of the hill sides pouring into it. The gorse (whins) was covered with its yellow flowers, which is in bloom the year round and the sides of the river were studded with majestic poplars. The drooping willow and the flax plants reminding me forcibly of those pictures in our Missionary presents of those Eastern Countries "where every prospect pleases and only man is vile". Soil – some of it very rich but a great quantity almost worthless. The great drawback to the land is that beneath are beds of shingle of several feet in depth. A farmer took me into one of his paddocks (fields are all called paddocks in N.Z.) and beneath a soil of 16 inches there was a clean shingle bed of 9 feet, and he told me in a dry season this land was as bare as the back of his hand. Otherwise the soil is light and clean and rarely a stone to be seen. With a wheeled plough the farmer can read a book or newspaper on the stilts of his plough all day long. Vegetables grow to a large size and potato disease is unknown but the land produce sells for very little at present.'

WORK & WAGES 'Having read Agent General's Hand Book and Rev. J. Berry's Pamphlet, I expected statements therein made as to abundance of work, high wages etc and general prosperity of New Zealand to be true. What was our surprise on landing to find hundreds walking the streets who could not get a day's work. Prospect being so dark we saw the necessity of moving very cautiously and having taken a four roomed house at 12/- per week in advance, purchased £6.10, worth of furniture and a cwt of coal for 3/-, we started housekeeping although in poor heart. Albert got work at a boot factory at 1/- per day. Willie called upon the builders and only one gave him any hope. This putting-off disposition found everywhere prevailing, was simply disgusting after the straight-forwardness we had been used to at home. "Get the smell of lime juice and pea soup off you and then call again". Willie's first engagement was three days as a pantryman at a restaurant called "His Lordship's Larder", next about three weeks serving a stone breaking machine and afterwards 3 months ploughing with Mr Boon a farmer at Riccarton, 6 miles from Christchurch, for which he was paid 10/- per week and tucker.

'John Tom was first employed hawking scones and pastry for a baker on commission, but could make nothing at it. Afterwards he got a fortnight's work at the stone-breaking machine, and then at Mr. King's soap works at 15/- per week. Having gone round the City and been unsuccessful, I called upon the Rev. Mr. Reid and presented my credentials. I called upon the employers whose addresses he gave me, they took my address and promised if they had or heard of anything they would inform me. Called again and again, offered to work hard for a boy's wages at anything, but never could get an engagement. During the six months we were there I was in turn cobbler, painter and carpenter but only for a casual day, and only earned 12/- in the country. I know of nothing that knocks the man out of you and makes you feel so despicable in your own sight as when looking at wife and children and being powerless to help them. I felt thoroughly miserable and determined to do anything that was honest. Went out one day with my tools soliciting lamps to repair and earned 3d. Went out two days seeking houses to paint, leaving addressed envelopes with the people, also advertised for painting but got nothing.

'As a soup kitchen was being opened called on the Mayor of Christchurch explaining my position and asking if a man would be required there. He enquired what my wife was doing and if she could not go out to or take in work to help us. I replied that after cooking, washing, mending and housekeeping for a family of 8 she could not be expected to do more, to which he replied

"Oh, I have known women with larger families make a lot of money sewing, etc". I could not say to him what I felt at such ungallantry, but my manly spirit stirred within me and as I turned away the thought that in the prime of life I should have, when willing to do anything I could, to depend on the earnings of my wife, caused the tears to gush from my eyes.'

I feel I must briefly interrupt the diarist to explain to the modern reader why John Hillary felt so keenly about it being suggested that his wife should do some work. At that time, with the exception of the very poor, married women just did not do anything but run the home and bring up the family. It must also be remembered that there were none of the labour-saving devices known today, and housework really was hard labour, and families much larger. Added to this was the fact that in Victorian times the husband was literally the breadwinner; any thought of the wife having to work was an insult to his manhood, and a slur on his ability to earn enough to keep the family. Certainly nobody in the diarist's position in life would allow such a thing.

'The soup kitchen is open daily by a committee with the Mayor at its head, who also distribute coal, clothing etc. to the suffering. Meetings of hundreds of unemployed are held in the Cathedral Square almost daily, who are signing petitions to the United States and Canadian Governments asking them to send a ship for the hundreds who are bordering on starvation. Much indignation is freely expressed, several of the more conscientious tradesmen joining, and the newspapers publishing letters and leaders charging home upon the Government the inconsistency of inveighling people away from their comfortable English homes by means of exaggerated and one sided lectures and pamphlets, to sorrow, untold suffering, disappointment and almost despair.

'A clerk, a new chum, not being able to get work took to book hawking and the day he called upon us he said that from that day week, he had not taken a penny. Another clerk called about the same time who having been out 15 months and got nothing, was trying to sell vinegar at a small commission. Another, Mr. W.

NEW ZEALAND

Raine, had only had a few hours carrying the monkey for the masons and returned with Mr. Williams on the S.S. "Cotopax". A very respectable man named Hawkes, an ironworker from Sunderland, having after paying passage for self and family out and being in Christchurch for months and never having a days work resolved, rather than stop and be totally ruined, also to return. He had just sufficient to pay ocean fare and intended asking the rail company at London to keep their luggage as security and send them on free home until they could raise the money and redeem their luggage.

'Met a family of father, mother and two sons who paid their passage and came out from Bradford shortly after us. They were printers to trade and had been in one of the best establishments in England at a good salary, had read the pamphlets and were persuaded. It was pityful to hear their regrets. Could not get a day's work and took to hawking tea, but found this a played-out game and next door to begging. The older son, who was a widower, with much emotion and tears, told me they would never settle and be happy until they were home again, and if friends in Bradford only knew their positon they would subscribe to pay their passage back. Mother was out at work and at harvest time the three men would go up country harvesting, work hard and save every penny until they could raise passage money.

'On July 3rd I had a conversation with Mr. Wallas, a bootmaker in the Colombo Rd. who came out 6 years ago and although the eldest son had made his way his large family scattered, some up country at farm stations whom he seldom heard of, and he finished by saying he would rather have England with one meal than all New Zealand had to offer. Mr. Mets, a shopkeeper in Colombo Rd. who is a general dealer showed me his takings, and on the first 3 days of July he only took 2/11d and seldom more than 35/- per week while his rent and gas amounted to 34/- per week without rates, thus leaving him with only 1/- to buy goods and keep his family. He said it was no good crying. I met a man in Christchurch who came out to Wellington also from Bradford, a short while before us, where he gave up a good tinsmith's business. He brought a patent machine for making tins and £700 in cash. When I met him he had lost all his money and been at Weka Pass where, although he had a family left at Bradford, he was paid 21/- per week and had nothing left to send home.

'A Mr. Sykes told me of a man from Hull whom he knew, a carpenter to trade, who could earn 50/- per week at home. He came out here and is now at Weka Pass at 21/- per week. Their bread having run out he and another went to a "Station" but instead of receiving the "proverbial hospitality" the Rev. J. Berry speaks of, they were neither given any food nor allowed to go near a fire and turned into a hen roost for the night.

'On September 1st I called at five places asking for employment, and Mr. Taylor, ironmonger, of Cashel St. told me he was from Canada. Several friends, for years, pressed him to advise them to come out to New Zealand, but he would never advise one of them, even in New Zealand's best days. When he was on a visit to Canada a few years ago a gentleman met him and asked his advice. Mr. T. told him if he could float at home he was to give up all thought of New Zealand. He was a gentleman worth some £10,000, and strange to say he sold out, spent all his capital in chartering a little ship, loading her with agricultural implements, which with his family he brought out. When he arrived in New Zealand the farmers would not look at his implements and scouted the idea that if they were adapted to Canada they were suitable for New Zealand. Mr. T. says the last he heard of him he was sitting on the rocks on the sea shore crying like a child, without a shilling left, ruined.

'The Agent General's "Hand Book" and the Rev. Berry's pamphlet, when they state the wages in New Zealand, should also in all truthfulness state that men do well who work three days per week and that most men are only half timers, and many work hard for a time and never receive any wages. The following facts which were given me prove this. A shipmate of ours, a mason named Davies, finished his first contract at building chimnies and his boss filed his petition and swindled him out of his earnings. I met a man this afternoon, Sept. 3rd who came out on the "Orari" 13 months ago. All the work he had was 3 months with a threshing machine for which he was to receive £1 per week and tucker. Unlike home, they don't profess to pay a man until the job is finished, and when he went to seek his wages his boss was "up a tree" and he never got a penny. When the gallery was put into Colombo Rd. church, where we attended,

NEW ZEALAND

two carpenters took the contract for the whole and sublet the plasterers and painters work. The painters were of course the last to finish and on the day following the two carpenters drew the whole £600, and filed their petition swindling the plasterers and painters out of every penny.

'Mr. Wilson, curer and leather merchant, also told me that during the last three years he had lost £3,000 and £1,000 during the last nine months by bankrupts who never paid 1d in the pound. Mr. Butcher, a London man, a bricklayer, told me his house was in his wife's name and when I asked the reason he said he was obliged to have it thus so that when people for whom he worked "filed", merchants could not come upon him for material. Mr. Millar, who has 8 houses in King St., the street we lived in, was building the 9th when we left. All his property is in his wife's name and every bit of wood he gets she has to stand for. He has gone through the courts so many times that when he made his last appearance the Judge told him that next time he appeared there he would inflict the highest penalty in his power for fraudulent bankruptcy.

'To show what those lecturers who came over to advocate New Zealand care for the people whom they induce to go out, Mr. Gibson a gentleman from Scotland who came from Dunedin on the "John Elder" told me of a minister named Isis who was over in England and Scotland advocating New Zealand some time ago. Two men, one of whom was a manager of a Co-Op store in Manchester followed Isis out. Mr. G. says that the last time he saw that man he was going about the streets of Dunedin with a bag picking up pieces of potato and coal to make a fire and roast the potatoes to keep body and soul together. The other man, starving, found the Rev. Isis out and asked him what he could do for him; he turned his back and cooly said "Nothing". Sorry to have thus to speak of Ministers, but what respect can we have left for men who will so disgrace the sacred office as to stoop for money to such disreputable work.

'Of the passengers who went out with us very few had any work when we left. Mr. Howard, from Consett, had only had about 12 day's work in an office. Mr. Richards only got a casual day's work now and again. His wife has been confined and he had been idle for three weeks and reduced to the last shilling, but a shipmate had given him 2/-. When in our house his blood boiled when speaking of the Rev. J. Berry who had by a letter advised him out, as he also did me. Mr. G. Rogers, a carpenter from London, having had very little work, had been obliged to sell a brooch and earrings value £3 which were presented to Mrs. R., who was a Wesleyan teacher trained at Westminster, and had recently been an accountant in a warehouse in London.

'A Mr. Spencer who told me he was willing and able to do a day's work with pick and shovel against any man, but could not get a living in the country. He had been up the country at 8/- per day and with loss of time through wet weather, difficulty in getting material for want of roads etc. after paying for his tucker, he brought home to wife and large family £4 for six weeks, which after paying 8/- per week for two rooms and 2/6 per cwt. for coal left them 2/10 per week to keep the lot. He added that he could do far better at home with 3/6 per week, and wished me to publish his statement. He also said the Agent General on this side seemed very particular about character, but in New Zealand his testimonials were never looked at, and the biggest scoundrel was in as good a turn as the most respectable man. Mr. Phillips left a situation at 50/- per week and never got any work in New Zealand. When we left he was swagging up country and wrote his wife saying he had forded three rivers in one of which he was nearly drowned, he was still wandering and had got nothing. I never saw such an object of distress as Mrs. P. was. Her eyes were sunk into her head, she had pawned her wedding ring to buy the little girl a pair of boots, and expected butcher and baker to stop supplies daily. She said if all Christchurch was her own she would give it to get back to Old England again.'

There is no doubt that John Hillary was very unlucky, and arrived in New Zealand at the time of the worst depression that country has ever known. The gold rush had subsided and the price of wool, which was the country's chief and almost only export, had fallen heavily on world markets. Being an up and coming country many goods were required from outside and while imports were rising exports were falling rapidly, creating a balance of payments problem. Thus money was leaving the country and little foreign money returning to replace it. World financiers were losing confidence in New Zealand's future and were withdrawing their capital as quickly as possible. Had John Hillary been a man who had mixed in financial circles there is little doubt he would have been made aware of the true position and not undertaken such a journey at that time. On the other hand being only a tradesman in a small and not very prosperous community he felt he could improve his position in a new country.

We must at least admire his courage and determination to succeed. In later years members of his family were to criticize him for returning so quickly and not staying and facing the position. It can be argued that it was in fact unfortunate he was able to find the money to pay for the entire family to return. Had he not been able to do this, he would have been forced to stay and see the thing through, but under the circumstances as he found them, to have chosen to remain would have required great courage, and it was a hard decision to make. How John Hillary found sufficient funds to pay for the passage home is not known to me, but it is most likely he had left enough money behind with his brother in Bishop Auckland and it was from there the necessary finance was sent. After all he was not a poor man; his business in Tow Law had not failed and there must have been money left over from the sale. Contrast his position with the young man on the 'Westland' who was robbed of £2, his sole capital, and we must wonder how he fared on arrival; at least he had no wife or family to support. It is doubtful if many or even any of the other immigrants were in the fortunate position of being able to return. Their descendants must be in New Zealand to this day which adds some weight to the view that the diarist should have tried to 'stick it out'.

John Hillary was not to know of an invention which in the space of the next ten years was to put New Zealand on its feet again. This was the advent of the refrigerated ship, the first of which, the 'Dunedin', sailed from Port Chalmers in February 1882. This enabled New Zealand to export her frozen mutton and also her dairy produce, thus giving a new prosperity which continues to this day. Strange to relate John Hillary's brother later left Bishop Auckland for New Zealand and remained there. Thus the name Hillary is known in that country to this day and in fact throughout the entire world, by the exploits of several of New Zealand's famous sons.

But to return to the diary we find the diarist now thoroughly disillusioned and very bitter against the Rev. J. Berry who had induced him to immigrate into New Zealand sitting by the river and near to tears because he could not make his way in such a lovely country.

Homeward Bound

And so the Hillary family leave 'The promised land' with no reference this time to 'Such expressions of respect etc' but we can imagine they left with no regrets and with a sense of great relief. After six months' struggle to find work and with no prospect of a happier future they must have been pleased to get started on the homeward journey. They were not sailing to England direct, and it was necessary for them to travel in a small coastal steamer to Australia and from there catch the larger vessel which would take them all the way back. Unlike the 'Westland' they were to call at several ports and for part of the journey were to retrace the outward voyage but under what different circumstances. On the way out there was the pleasure of anticipating what the future had in store and the prospect of possible success in a new land. Now this was all gone and it must have been with feelings of sadness and frustration John Hillary once more goes on board ship. The only advantage this time being that each day was one day nearer home and to his beloved class.

WESTLAND

RETURN VOYAGE FROM NEW ZEALAND

Tuesday 7th September 1880. 'Left Christchurch by the 2.40 pm train and Lyttelton at 4 pm on board the Union Company's S.S. "Tararua" a dirty but strong and seaworthy coasting ship. Were all rather sick especially the children.'

The 'Tararua' was classed as an Iron Screw Steamer, built by Gourley Bros. Dundee in 1864. She was approximately the same size as the 'Westland' being the same length but somewhat narrower beam, and did not rely entirely on the engine but had three masts on which sails were hoisted under favourable wind conditions. She was wrecked some six months later in very tragic circumstances on Waipapapa Reef New Zealand with the loss of 102 lives including women and children (see appendix).

Wednesday 8th September. 'Arrived at Port Chalmers at 1.30 p.m. and remained overnight in the harbour.'

Thursday 9th September. 'Left Port Chalmers at 3.pm having taken on board a lot of passengers who are returning home quite disgusted with the state of things existing in Otago.'

Friday 10th September. 'At 7.am. we landed at the Bluff, the port for Invercargil. Here a Danish woman in Mamma's cabin presented her husband with two little stowaways. The Bluff is a miserable looking place, the moorland round it much resembling Hedley Hill banks. We left there about 2.pm., passed through Foveaux Strait where we had a good view of the lower end of Otago and Stewart Island and soon getting into lumpy water our passengers one after the other felt as though they had dined off german yeast and began to cast up their accounts and such a night we passed for storm, rolling and pitching as I hope never again to experience. The strong old "Tararua" laboured so heavily and the seas struck her with such force that she shook from stem to stern and we feared we would be dashed to pieces.'

Saturday 11th September. 'Very few can appear at breakfast table this morning and these holding on by both hands to their bunks and looking amazed as though they were just coming out of a terrible nightmare. A very stormy day and tempestuous sea. So far, our passage has been a very rough one even for the coast of New Zealand with its reputation for storms and where so many lives have been lost.'

Sunday 12th September. 'Rather better weather and a few got on deck, but they were poorly. J.W. (John Willy) says if he had not booked through he would have had no more of it but stopped at Melbourne, so tired is he of the voyage already, it makes him so ill. The wind having shifted from the head to the port side we have got some sail on, and the old boat does not roll so much. What joy it is to be journeying home to old England the land of Christian privileges and Christian Sabbaths. I could wish the weeks without Sabbaths such as they are, for they only give me pain, but a few more and I shall regain them in their sweetness in my dear old house.'

Monday 13th September. 'Had beef and potatoes to breakfast. A very wet uncomfortable morning. Going about 10 knots per hour. Old Jack Taranacki, a passenger is very ill and calling for some canvas to stitch him up in. No wonder, for yesterday he only consumed 2 bottles of lemonade and a tin of sardines all the oil of which he drank because the steward told him it would make him strong. He is very ill and groaning like a dying horse. A gale springing up at noon the sea is again running dangerously high.'

Tuesday 14th September. 'Had a terrible night and all were much alarmed. Heavy seas were shipped and in one of them tons of water must have been heaved on deck by the furious elements for the shock nearly sent us all out of our bunks and the old steamer trembled under it for some time. All are lightheaded this morning. A passenger missing a tall gentlemanly looking man. He kept in his bunk all yesterday suffering from neuralgia and we think that either the rheumatism has struck his desperate brain and made him a suicide or having occasion to go on deck during the stormy night, when sailors could only with difficulty keep their feet, a sea struck him overboard. As he is not now on board the only sad alternative is he is added to the myriads who are buried beneath the wild, wild waves. From a pocketbook found in his overcoat it appears his name is Michael Carr, he has been sixteen years farming at Leeston near Christchurch where he has left his wife and children. Having cleared out, he was on his way to Victoria to buy land and make a home. The storm has abated. Passed Tasmania in the evening.'

John Hillary and family are now well and truly homeward bound which must have been some consolation for the stormy weather they immediately encountered. Indeed the weather seems to have been even worse than their passage through the Bay, for the diarist expresses more alarm on this occasion, even though he was by now a seasoned traveller having had the experience of three months at sea. Previously he had never been on the water. They had to retrace their outward journey round Otago coast and through the Forveaux Strait and passing Stewart Island but this time they made several stops which must have given great relief from the storm. Having rounded South Island they would turn North and continue to Australia passing Tasmania on the way. This journey occupied nine days.

Wednesday 15th September. 'A fine morning and a calm sea, a double quantity of edibles consumed at breakfast table. At 10.am we are on the coast of Gipps-Land which is ninety miles from the Heads, and 130 from Melbourne. At 5.pm we have a fine view of the Australian coast from opposite Shag Point. It is not so rugged as the coast of New Zealand. At 7.pm we entered the harbour and were tugged up the Yarra to the wharf which we reached at midnight, glad to step on terra firma once more.'

Thursday 16th September. 'Took lodging at The London and Carnarvon Hotel at 17/- per day, best we could do. Uncle Richardson came to see us in the evening.'

Australia has the distinction of being the largest island in the world and the only continent in the Southern Hemisphere. Melbourne is the capital of the state of Victoria. Our travellers must have been very grateful to find accommodation at The London & Carnarvon Hotel. There is no mention of how they fared there but by the scant reference it would seem not too well.

At least the beds would be stationary which was something they had not enjoyed for the last nine nights. The price of 17/- per day would seem to cover all of them – it certainly would not be per person – which gives some idea of the value of money at that time. It would appear that John Hillary had relatives in Australia as we read of 'Uncle Richardson' but the writer has no knowledge of these. As will be seen the next few days were spent on visiting relatives though the diarist omits any entry for Friday the 17th and Sunday the 19th. Mention is made of 'The Diggings' but as in New Zealand the golden age was a thing of the past.

Saturday 18th September. 'Went at Uncle's expense to Newlyn, John James meeting us at Daylesford station with their buggy and a drive of 11 miles brought us to their pleasantly situated and hospitable home, where Robert and John Richardson came to see us and enquire after the welfare of all Tow Law friends.'

Monday, 20th September. 'Returned to Melbourne, James drove us through the diggings 7 miles to Creswick, a pretty village where Robert Richardson came 4 miles in his buggy to see us off and brought us a large fine home-fed ham for use on the ship. Stopped 3 hours at Ballarat, a good sized well built and clean town and about half an hour at Geelong where C.T. Richardson met us. Geelong is also a town of considerable size, but of course in all these places the activity and excitement is a thing of the past. After travelling by this route 170 miles we reached Melbourne at 4.pm. Victoria is very much like the North of England but not comparable to New Zealand for beauty.'

Tuesday 21st September. 'Went on board the "John Elder" the fine steamship of the Pacific Steam Navigation Company at 9.am and at 12 noon started upon our return voyage to old England. Passengers were beside Britons, Germans, Italian, Swedes, Frenchmen, 1 Norwegian and 1 Arab. The Frenchmen who had been exiled after the Franco-Prussian war to New Caledonia for 10 years and their term having expired, were returning to Paris.'

The 'John Elder' was built by J. Elder & Co, Glasgow and completed in August 1870. Gross Tons: 4,160. Length: 406 ft, breadth: 41.5 ft. Compound Steam Engine of 550 HP. For further details see appendix and the diarist's entry dated 4th October.

Wednesday 22nd September. 'Strong head wind and rough sea. It was very dangerous venturing on deck during the day, but the night was a terror for storm. The sheep, pigs and cattle suffered severely, indeed some of the bullocks had their lives almost knocked out of them. A seaman had his shoulder dislocated and a passenger some ribs broken and one boat was smashed.'

The Hillary family were certainly having their share of stormy weather and there was more to come towards the end of the voyage. It is unlikely that stabilizers would be fitted to the 'John Elder' so the sufferings of the passengers must have been quite severe; the more so as we have reason to believe our travellers would be in what was then known as 'Steerage'. This as the word implies was in the extreme stern of the ship just over the screw and rudder where most of the motion and noise would be experienced. At least the passengers had the advantage of knowing what it was all about but what of the poor dumb animals which had to be carried to provide fresh meat. Their suffering must have been appalling. A small but interesting point is the use of the expression 'A terror for storm' a colloquialism then in use in New Zealand and after only six months already acquired by the diarist.

Thursday 23rd September. 'Tempest still raging and a strong adverse wind hinders progress. Four bullocks in a dying state were killed for their hides and their bruised and blackened carcasses thrown to the sharks.'

Friday 24th September. 'Early this morning arrived in Adelaide harbour and cast anchor glad to find shelter from the stormy weather of the Australian coast and the perils of the great deep.'

Saturday 25th September. 'A busy day taking in passengers, cargo and coal. Sad accounts by passengers of the state of the colonies. One young man from Nottingham has only been out six months, earned but £5 swagging and lying in canvas tents and is a loser by £90. A family from Staffordshire named Davies have been eight months in Wellington and they will be £400 out before they get home. A mason from Haswell has been two years in Sydney and Melbourne doing sinking or anything else and is obliged to return because he cannot live. A young man from Belper who left home two days before us and has been swagging in New Zealand is also returning. He tells me he has spent £350, and a very respectable man named Terrell a wheelwright, who has lived near Adelaide for 20 years is returning with wife and seven children to London, disgusted with the discomforts and uncertainties of colonial life. This evening a boat came alongside bringing us 8 bullocks; they were a savage lot and had killed one man in capture. Seven of them were hoisted on deck by steam winch and a rope round their horns, but the 8th slipped out and swam ashore again. All busy making ready for a start.'

Sunday 26th September. 'Early this morning we set sail again and soon got into lumpy water with a strong head wind. Ship heaves very much. We have had a rough passage so far, Lord of the Sabbath bring us safety home.'

Monday 27th September. 'Sea somewhat settled during the night and today we are going along smartly yet pleasantly at 12 miles an hour. Had a conversation on deck with a man who came out from Preston in Lancashire eleven months ago and left a situation of £2 per week upstanding. He returns with a deficit of £90 and is thankful he left wife and two children at home. He had 5 months work for which he got wages and afterwards 3 months of heavy wet work, but when he went to draw his wages his boss was "Up a tree" and he got nothing.'

Tuesday 28th September. 'A strong side wind is propelling the "John Elder" swiftly along but a nasty sea is running. Killed the lean calf and two sheep and cast another bullock overboard.'

Wednesday 29th September. 'Wind light but fair, clear sky, weather warm and pleasant. Oh for "Home sweet home" and some employment, a life of idleness is to me a life of misery.'

Thursday 30th September. 'A great change of weather, strong wind and heavy sea. Ship labours heavily and staggers under the heavy seas which strike her. I was greatly distressed during the night, having dreamed that Jonathan Hodgson had been killed by a fall of stone in the pit. I sympathized with his family.'

There is an interesting entry here regarding the death of Jonathan Hodgson. The writer has every reason to believe that this event did in fact take place on that day and in the manner stated. This is made more curious by the fact that Jonathan Hodgson, as far as I know, was not even a relative but in a small community was no doubt well known to the diarist. Perhaps he was a member of John Hillary's Tuesday Bible Class. Be that as it may, such phenomena are still being investigated today, without as yet any feasible explanation.

Friday 1st October. '"Rocked in the cradle of the deep." I am sick of the sea and wish we had been rolling up the Thames this morning. Day got out fine but cold. Killed a bullock, sheep and a pig. Have passed Cape Luin.'

Saturday 2nd October. 'Fine sailing weather. I blacked all the children's boots and my own. Doing 300 miles a day.'

John Hillary in his account of the homeward journey no longer gives the daily mileage. Here we have recorded 'Doing 300 miles a day' against which we have the highest days run by the 'Westland' of 306 (29/11/79). But the 'John Elder' could maintain this speed day after day whereas the 'Westland' could not, hence the decline of sail. At the same time it would appear from the entry on October 4th that even the 'John Elder' used sails when the wind was favourable.

There must have been an improvement in the weather for we have a return to the mention of 'Godless Sabbaths' and on

HOMEWARD BOUND

Tuesday October 5th to his Bible Class. Perhaps the stormy weather had kept his mind on more immediate matters as this is almost the only reference to religious affairs since leaving New Zealand.

Sunday 3rd October. 'A Sunday but no sabbath. Oh, for one Tow Law Sabbath. What a Godless place this is. The regulations say this Holy Day is to be kept as religiously as circumstances will permit. I see no change either in work or wickedness. Morning Captain read prayers in the first saloon and evening a cursing steward officiated in the steerage, but I did not attend and countenance such blasphemy, for how can blessing and cursing proceeding out of the same lips glorify God. Fine breeze. Warmer weather. Pleasant day.'

Monday 4th October. 'A warm morning and very little wind, yet such is the advantage of steam as well as sails we are going rapidly. The "John Elder" is a fine built steamer, 150 yds long, fitted with hurricane decks. Draws 25 ft under water and has three decks above it. Has 24 fireholes and 27 firemen and consumes 50 tons of coal per day. Carries 450 souls, including officers and crew, £156,000 in specie, thousands of bales of wool and 2,000 tons of coal, besides other valuables making her cargo one of the most precious ever brought from Australia.'

Tuesday 5th October. 'A fine day and propitious wind. How on these Tuesday evenings do I long for the sweet fellowship of God's people in class assembled.'

Wednesday 6th October. 'Weather becoming hot. Killed a bullock a sheep and a pig. Albert has gone to assist the saloon cook, his remuneration being better "tucker" for self, Father and Mother. This is very acceptable, the rations of the third class being uneatable. A lot of us waited upon the Captain and Chief Steward this morning taking a sample of the greasy rice served up for our breakfast and requesting that in future the boiled rice may be sweetened with sugar instead of being boiled with fat meat. The Captain promised our request should be granted. As very little was eaten that remaining was given to the pigs but they pitched it out of their troughs and with a grunt turned up their snouts. A passenger at sea should have stomach like a sausage machine, able to digest anything.'

How inferior the food appears to have been on the 'John Elder' compared with the outward voyage where there is frequent mention of good and plentiful food. It seems strange that the meals would seem to have been so bad on the return journey because the Hillarys were no longer emigrants but fare paying passengers. One would have expected the reverse to be the case. They were lucky to get Albert working in the galley and we can only hope things improved as expected. A point of interest is that on the 'Westland' they cooked their own food.

Thursday 7th October. 'After a hot night and little sleep have cast off drawers, stockings and flannel shirt. Saw about 100 flying fish in one shoal this morning, they are only to be seen in warm latitudes.'

Friday 8th October. 'Excessively hot and the nights bring but little relief. Sailing about 300 miles daily. The Arab passenger, Ab Dallah, who has been ill since leaving Adelaide, died at noon and at 1.pm a respectable looking Irishman took a fit on deck and is very ill from Excessive heat. Yet who cares for sickness and death on board ship so long as they themselves are well, no one sheds a tear or heaves a sigh. "Has he any money?" I overheard a passenger smilingly ask the Frenchman who acted as attendant and interpreter to the Arab as he came out of the hospital when the last offices were performed and the spirit had fled. "Here is the coffin" cries the sailmaker with a laugh as he jaunts along the deck with the canvas on his shoulder. "Have you got the cold meat stitched up yet," asks a steward in derision, as though he himself was immortal. As the law requires that corpses at sea be buried within 2 hours, at 2.pm this poor disciple of a Mahomet was without a sigh or a tear or a funeral note, the engines merely stopping for a minute and the sailors raising their caps, committed to the great grave of the Indian Ocean. Which I am told is 11,000 miles long, 10,000 broad and averaging 4 miles in depth.

'A Welshman named Broad, in the next cabin to ours has been in New Zealand and New South Wales for 5 years and never had a chair to sit upon. He says he sometimes returned home from work so exhausted by hard toil and heat that he could not unfasten his shoes, until health and strength failed and the doctor told him if he worked 6 weeks more he would be in his grave. At 28 years he looks 40 and returns home, I fear, to die. He tells me he knows two men who went out to New Zealand, one being a schoolmaster at home with 12 children and the other a postman with 10 children. He says he never saw men so disappointed. Not being able to get work they bought canvas tents and went into the bush where all working they could hardly get salt. The schoolmaster sometimes did painting when he could get it, or anything else, but they were almost reduced to starvation.'

Saturday 9th October. 'Oh that we were out of this tropical heat it is like a oven, melting the marrow in the bones. Left my bed and spent the night on deck.'

Sunday 10th October. 'Heat is terrific too much for animal life. Captain read prayers in the saloon at 10.30 and in the evening a service was read in the third class quarters. Two women fainted and a bullock was to kill on account of the heat. One of the women is very ill. Passengers had to leave their berths and were lying all over the deck but this gave little relief as the midnight air was so hot we could hardly breath.'

Monday 11th October. 'Just sufficient clothing for decency. Yet the heat is almost like a furnace, Edith is very sick and poorly and has all the symptoms of Tropical fever. A splendid Eastern sunset.'

Tuesday 12th October. 'Thankful Edith is better. At 11.30 am we crossed the Line and are in the Eastern Hemisphere again. Slept on deck. Killed two sheep and one bullock. Speed away Tuesday evenings and bring me to better society for this is a prayless and Godless place.'

On this day they crossed the Line again and we find no reference to any sort of ceremony. This seems strange as this was a passenger liner and one would have thought some attention would have been drawn to their crossing the Equator. True the diarist was only travelling 3rd class but no mention is made of any revels, even among the first class passengers. It is fairly certain John Hillary would have mentioned these if any had taken place. It would certainly seem that nothing special was done to mark this occasion in those days as even on the 'Westland' no notice was taken of this event.

Wednesday 13th October. 'Heat less oppressive, Edith and all the other sick ones better. Expect to reach Aden on Sunday. This evening we had another of those tropical and oriental panoramas which time will never blot from memory's page. Oh that I had the power to describe the scene. The sun is setting in blood, his background a clear blue sky, his curtains pink, scarlet, rose, magenta crimson, amber, yellow and all the imaginable hues, while clouds like forest trees are piled on either side. The glorious glaxy of the stellar heavens "Worlds upon worlds amazing pomp" the sea like a sheet of glass. Flying fish in scores skating on the placid water, shoals of large porpoises gambolling near the ship's side, all fill my soul with a profound reverence for the great Creator and remind me of the majestic lines of Pollock:–
   Whose garments were the clouds,
   Whose minstrels brooks, whose lamps the moon and stars,
   Whose angel choirs the voice of many waters,
   Whose bouquets, morning dews, whose heroes storms,
   Whose warriors, mighty winds, whose lovers, flowers,
   Whose orators, the thunderbolts of God,
   Whose palaces, the everlasting hills,
   Whose ceiling, heavens unfathomable blue.

Thursday October 14th. 'A further diminution of the heat as we leave the Equator but we may expect a recurrence in the Red Sea. A good wind and a pleasant sailing. A day's sail nearer home, what a joyful thought. Have just finished after three days, reading the life of that noble man John Ashworth of Rochdale.'

Thinking it would be interesting to discover John Hillary's taste in literature and as the name John Ashworth was quite unknown to me I wrote to Rochdale for help. The Director of the

Rochdale Libraries and Arts Services, Mr. G.E. Thornber supplied the following information.

'John Ashworth was born on the 8th July 1813 the son of a woollen weaver, he became the minister at the Chapel for the Destitute which he founded after a visit to London had revealed to him the suffering of the poor. As an author, pamphleteer and traveller, he acquired a world wide reputation and popularity which remained with him until his death on the 26th January, 1875.'

Mr. Thornber also mentions a book by A.L. Calman 'Life and labours of John Ashworth', published in 1875 and it seems fairly certain this would be the edition the diarist was reading. To my surprise a book has been published as recently as 1972 by Gospel Tidings Publications entitled simply 'John Ashworth'.

Friday 15th October. 'A sea of glass, a bright blue sky, a burning sun, whales blowing up, flying and jelly fish in abundance, truly we are in the tropics. At 8 pm passed Cape Guardafin off the coast of Africa and in the moonlight had a good view of the rocky shore. Here some time ago 5 ships having gone too near the shore were plundered by the natives. Met two fishing smacks carrying bright lights.'

Saturday 16th October 'Fine but very sultry morning. Met and passed a ship at 8 am. Are now in the Gulf of Aden but as we don't require coal are not going to call there. The bright moonlight seems to inspire our passengers, for music, dancing and fencing by the Frenchmen was carried on to a late hour on deck.'

Sunday 17th October. 'Scarcely a breath of air and the heat is worse than ever this morning. At 2 am passed Aden and at 10 am passed through Hells Gate or the Strait of Babel Mandeb having a good view of the coasts of Mocha Arabia on the right or Asiatic side and Abyssinia on the left or African side. An exciting time for after having seen only one ship in the Indian Ocean for three weeks, we met and passed in the Strait 4 steamers and 3 little boats with sails set. One of the latter had a lot of Africans on board in an almost nude state and from their savage looks I had no desire for any nearer acquaintance. At

The Wesleyan Chapel, Tow Law

The Hillary family pew and commemorative plaque inside the Wesleyan Chapel Tow Law

night the air was so hot the cabins below were like ovens and the deck was covered with people trying to sleep with only a covering over their faces to save them from moon blindness which in these parts is very dangerous. I managed to sleep 5 hours in a draught under a boat and Mamma and baby on the forecastle got a little sleep.'

We now have frequent mention of the terrible heat and of course there would be no air conditioning on the 'John Elder' nor refrigeration either. Not even cold drinks to ease the passengers' lot and sleep well nigh impossible. But if the passengers suffered what of the crew working deep in the vessel attending to the engines and boilers, with no automatic stokers – all the coal had to be shovelled into the furnaces by hand.

The reference to 'Moon Blindness' is interesting; it was the firm belief of the Victorian that this could result from the moonlight shining on the face when asleep. While the diarist managed 5 hours sleep 'Mamma' seems to have fared less well with baby on the fos'c'le. We read little about the family on this journey and can only surmise that life on the steamer was different and the family not so closely knit. On the outward voyage they had to look after themselves and were on a much smaller vessel.

Monday 18th October. 'Several ill of diarrhoea on account of the heat and no wonder, for the perspiration is running down our bodies although our dress is a near approach to that of our first parents. At 11 am the thermometer is 110 F in the shade. At 2 pm passed three steamers one of which was a fine large boat of the P & O Line. This is the hottest night we have had, even the little air we are getting off the African coast is as hot as though coming out of a furnace.'

Tuesday 19th October. 'We shall never forget the heat of the Red Sea. Our butcher says that six years ago he was coming this route on the S.S. Cusso when her machinery broke down and she was disabled. Prayers were offered up at port and she was given up, however, she managed to reach London in 160 days by the use of her sails. Just about where we are now many of her passengers succumbed to the heat including 10 in the second saloon. One man requested the Captain that should he die a good coffin should be made for him as he had a horror of being thrown overboard in canvass and the remainder of his money to be given to the Seaman's Widows & Orphans fund. At noon his body was found on the seat of the W.C. One gentleman feeling himself going passed his ring to a fellow passenger and in three days both occupied the same grave, the unfathomable deep. Am myself very poorly from the heat it seems too much for my weak constitution. Evening killed a bullock and three sheep. Are opposite Mecca in Arabia on the right and Nubia on our left.'

Wednesday 20th October. 'A head wind but cooler than if coming off the coast on either side. At noon passed two steamers and at 4 pm passed two islands called the Twin Brothers. At 12 pm had a fine moonlight view of the coast on either side as we are entering the Gulf of Suez having just passed Desolation Islands on the left. The dangers of the Red Sea on account of the coral rocks are many. Oh, my Lord, on the coast of Egypt I this night consecrate myself again to Thee and promise if Thou wilt guide me safely home that my life shall be fully devoted to Thee.'

Thursday 21st October. 'Stood on deck until 2 am watching the towering rocks and a revolving light on the coast of Egypt. This light was put up by the P & O Company on a projecting rock where one of their steamers was wrecked. The scenery is splendid in the early morning as the Gulf gets narrower up to Suez. At 8 am we passed 4 steamers. The Irishman before mentioned had another fit on deck this morning. Our afflictions are never so great but we see others who have greater, how thankful I am I never had a fit. I am looking into the sea for some of Pharaoh's chariot wheels as we must be very near the spot where the Lord took them off Pharaoh's 600 chosen chariots of Egypt with which the Israelites were pursued. Got out my bible and as I sat on deck reading the history of that miraculous interposition, Exodus 14/15, with the place before my eyes readers judge what my feelings were. Perpendicular rocks 60/100 ft high and between them a plain of sand for about 50 yards, I could fancy God's chosen people standing in the aperture and lifting up their eyes over the sand desert behind them and seeing their enemies pursuing them turning upon the meek Moses and derisively saying "Because there were no graves in Egypt hast thou taken us away to die in the wilderness". And I could almost hear the hoary prophet saying "Fear ye not stand still and see the salvation of the Lord which He will show you today." Then stretching out the rod and dividing the waters and the sacramental host of God's elect passing through dry shod.

'At 3 pm arrived at Suez and were immediately surrounded by about a dozen bumboats with Arabs and Gypsies displaying their wares, such as coral, shell necklaces, drink, apples, figs, pomegranates, salmon, sardines, tobacco, cigars etc; they did a good stroke of business especially in the brandy. Their modus operandi was for one of the men from each boat to climb by a rope like a monkey up the side of the ship and draw his wares in a basket as called for. They have black or bronze skins, wear turbans and long cotton gowns with a belt round the waist, white stockings and sandals. They speak a broken English except when speaking to each other and ask four times the value of every article.

'Suez is a little town about the size of Crook, the buildings looking clean and new. The pilot having boarded us at 4 pm we entered the Canal. The greatest attraction of this memorable day was the Arab boys, clad in Eden's luxury of dress viz; a rag to cover their nakedness, who ran by our side on the bank of the Canal for three or four miles crying "Backsheesh" money "Backsheesh". Biscuits, nuts, potatoes and coin were thrown them and in their eagerness to catch them they plunged up to the chin and performed curious antics in the water to the amusement of the saloon and nabob passengers especially. As it is not safe to navigate the Canal at night we anchored at 7 pm; in one of the sidings provided, for it is so narrow ships cannot pass, and the night being warm and moonlight fishing and bathing went on until late.'

To a person of such deep religious conviction this must have been a most wonderful experience. John Hillary firmly believed the Old Testament account (and who is to say he was wrong to do so) and to be passing the places where these things took place undoubtedly moved the diarist very deeply. It must have been exciting to John Hillary for the next day or two to see these biblical scenes passing before his eyes. Here was something to tell his class about on his return.

Friday 22nd October. 'Weighed anchor at 7 am but before starting a French Steamer passed us with hundreds of wretched, dirty Arabs who cheered us in passing. Their dress was a turban and a gown of dirty blue print and they were making the periodical pilgrimage to Mecca to perform the obligations of the Mahomedan religion, or rather delusion, for what more can it be which leaves its votaries so debased. Christianity raises men everywhere and in every respect but Mahomedanism leaves its disciples base in their morals dark in their minds and filthy in their persons. The coasts of Arabia on the right and Egypt on the left are, as far as the eye can see, nothing but rock, sand and barreness everywhere.

'Suez Canal is 93 miles long, is cut through the land of Goshen and varies in width from 50 yards to 5 or 6 miles where it goes through two lakes. It is worked by telegraphic communication and sidings are provided at intervals for steamers to wait in passing. In the narrow places great care is needed and we only went about 4 miles per hour, but in the lakes about 10 miles. On the banks on either side small native hamlets are springing up with their flat roofed, sand or concrete built houses of one storey some of which have small gardens and a few trees growing in them. Women are standing at the doors, at least such I took them to be, but their dress makes the sexes difficult to distinguish, children playing around, dogs lounging and goats grazing on the poor herbage on which only goats, donkeys and camels can subsist. One of these houses attracted attention particularly, standing on a small island with palm and other trees growing round it and fishing boats moored close by.

'At 1 pm passed near Ishmaelia. A drove of about 200 camels and 2 ponies in charge of a few Arabs on the right and camels bearing burdens with an Arab trudging by their sides on the left hand. (Scripture scenes rise). It is not unusual for large steamers to ground in the Canal, have to discharge cargo and be detained for days, however, we got through safely and reached Port Said about 10 pm. The town contains 3,000 inhabitants, Turks, Greeks, Arabs, Gypsies and Africans and has sprung up as an outcome of the Canal scheme. The people are low, cowardly, treacherous villains, living by barter, fraud and the wages of iniquity. Several of our male passengers went ashore for a night's debauch, but one of them told me on their return he felt sorry he had gone and witnessed such total moral depravity.

'The natives boarded our ship by scores displaying their wares in great variety and talking sanctimoniously of "Father Jacob" extorting as much from the passengers as they could and when money was done, change for change. The most amusing part of the affair was when a boat came alongside with a supply of water from the Nile, which empties itself here and 4 barges with 600 tons of coal. About 150 miserable wretches without shoes or stockings carried the coal in baskets on their shoulders and tipped them into the hold. All night long did their babble continue until few got any sleep. I suppose this was kept up to incite the idle scoundrels to work but two ganders fighting never made a greater row among a flock of geese and 50 Englishmen would have beaten them all for work. The coal was Welsh being kept here to supply passing steamers.'

This entry gives us an insight into the outlook of the Victorians. It must be remembered that at that time Great Britain was the premier nation in the world. It was the hey-day of the empire builders and there is no doubt Britons really did feel superior to all other people and especially to non-whites. Britain in the 1800's had shown the lead in the industrial revolution and this engendered a feeling of superiority which was then perhaps not entirely unjustified and this feeling was fostered in the schools by the way history was taught. There seems little doubt that the diarist, although he would have been shocked had he realised it, possessed this same outlook as is evidenced by his references to natives. These are classed as wretches, villains, scoundrels etc, and all up to devilish tricks.

At the same time it would seem that some of the whites in New Zealand were not beyond a little sharp practice now and again. It does not seem to have occurred to John Hillary that lack of opportunity, education and indeed sheer poverty could have been largely responsible for the apparent backwardness in these people and not the colour of their skins. Yet he is quite compassionate over the death of the Arab Ab Dallah, mentioned earlier, and thinking others callous but being unaware of intolerance in himself which we see also evinced in his attitude to religions other than Christianity. It did not occur to the diarist that at least these pilgrims were doing something for their religion misguided though that something might seem to him. Perhaps age mellowed him and after all he was only about 40 and no doubt had still a lot to learn and experience.

Saturday 23rd October. 'Resumed our journey at 6 am and passing Alexandria with the pillar called the Pharos on our left we were soon in European waters in the Mediterranean Sea. Weather fine and with good Welsh coal, which is 50% better than colonial, making only half the ashes and twice the steam, we are ripping through the ocean at great speed. Being now in the track of vessels we saw several large ships and steamers during the day. These are dull Saturday nights and increase the longing for home but I hope another will be the last on the sea. The temperature being now comfortable, I retired early to bed for rest and quiet thought, treacherous memory tantalized me with the remembrance of:–

"Hopes that were angels in their birth,
But perished soon like all of earth."

'A person on board from Scotland told me that he has been 21 years in Victoria and Gippsland but has had no home comforts. He says sunstroke is very common the thermometer sometimes being 104 F. in the shade in harvest time, and those having sunstroke once are always after mentally dull. He says mature life is from 27 to 30 years after which decline soon follows, that girls marry usually at 15 and can be seen with one child by the hand and another at the breast, the mother looking only like a school-girl herself.'

What a relief it must have been to leave the Canal behind and be sailing in the Mediterranean. The extreme heat being now abated it was possible to retire to bed again and not spend the nights on deck. To get into European waters only increased the diarist's longing to be home and the lines which he quotes suggest he had been thinking of his hopes and aspirations on the outward journey, now dashed for ever.

HOMEWARD BOUND

Sunday 24th October. 'Fine morning. Going at a rare speed. All thoroughly sick of the monotony of sea life and counting the days until we reach home. I am tired of the forced companionship of wicked men and meditating on the goodness of Him who led Joseph like a flock and has guided me my life long. Sacred as was the Temple to the Jews it had not more attractions than the old Chapel at home has for me, poor as it looks its hallowing influence does my heart good even now, both in the retrospect and the prospect. Although the Sabbath is to be observed as religiously as circumstances will permit, how this holy day is desecrated. Butcher washed out grain store, killed 2 sheep and 1 bullock and everything went on as on a week day.'

Monday 25th October. 'A rough sea, ship pitches heavily, several sick again. This evening the sky was dark, black clouds out of which lightning flashed ahead indicative of a coming storm. Everything moveable is lashed to the bulwarks and in a few minutes the storm is upon us. We had the electric light in reality the deck being flooded with light which quivered and lingered until the most stout hearted were afraid. Killed 6 sheep today.'

Tuesday 26th October. 'Very rough sea, white horses on each side after the storm last night truly we are "Rocked in the cradle of the deep" and all sickly. At 11 am 4 ships are in view and the coast of Italy discovering itself. What a pleasure to see European shores again. At 2 pm under the shelter of the coast the sea calm. A fine view of Reggio and some small villages, towering hills, creeks, vineyards and fruitful fields. Truly Italy is a land of beauty. But yet more beautiful still did some pronounce the coast of Sicily on our left with Messina in full view. At sunset we passed the Lipari Islands and Stromboli belching out its fire and smoke was so near that some of the children were afraid and asked if that was the place where all wicked people were to go. Am sorry Etna was too far away to descry plainly. The scenery of this day will never be forgotten by us.'

Wednesday 27th October. 'Another memorable day. Before daybreak we reached Naples the pride of Italy and reputedly the prettiest city in the world. Had a splendid view of Vesuvius in the dawn casting up smoke, fire and lava from its crater and on the other side of us the city as seen from the bay is most picturesque a perfect panorama. A railway train is drawn by a standing engine up the mountain side and quite a town of houses are clustered round its fertile base. Before anchor was cast scores of men and women were round us in their boats with baskets of fruit, wines and a variety of showy common jewellery. Several passengers went shore and were fleeced of money and virtue. The streets of the city are narrow but very clean being all paved and many having trees growing along their sides. The houses are generally five storeys high and very uniform. There are many fine public buildings and the whole standing upon rising ground is seen to advantage from the harbour. Resumed our voyage at 3 pm.'

Thursday 28th October. 'Captain Groves being now running against time and steaming at full power we have got a good rocking during the night. The oscillation from the propellers is so very unpleasant several again sick this morning. Sighted Sardinia at 11 am and passed opposite Cape Spartivento at 3 pm going 13 miles per hour. Sighted sometimes 4 ships at one time and so many during the day I did not think it necessary to mention them all separately. Of all the sights upon the sea that of a ship in full sail is the prettiest and landsmen can form no adequate conception of its beauty at a distance. When the ship is decked out in all her canvas and every sail swelled and careering gaily over the erratic waves, how lofty she looks, how gloriously her gallant course she goes, how she seems to lord it over the angry deep, moving apparently by her own volition and playing like a huge monster of the deep.
"She walks the water like a thing of life,
And dares the angry elements to strife".'

Friday 29th October. 'A rough sea which increased in severity as the day advanced and the afternoon is awfully tempestuous, seas breaking over us. The ship is almost standing still although her engines are working up to full power so strong is the wind and so high is the sea. Many passengers are looking alarmed "My fears are great my strength is small" Lord save us. I often doubt whether we shall reach home again.'

Saturday 30th October. 'Weather still very rough and everything wet and uncomfortable. The Spanish coast on our right very plainly in view, also 17 ships sighted at one time and 30 during the day besides 4 steamers going the same course as us. These we passed nearly together opposite Cape deGata about 4 pm. At 9 pm are opposite Malaga from whence a flash light is shining brightly. A stormy night.'

Sunday 31st October. 'Especially on Sabbath days do I feel most impatient to be away from the wicked practices and workers of iniquity. When I think of nearly 500 on this ship candidates for eternity how I feel for them yet all I can do is by my own example. My precepts only raise the jeers and the scoffs of the wicked and are as pearls before swine so I answer not a fool according to his folly. At 4 am was on deck and had a starlight view of the Rock of Gibralter as we passed through the strait. At 10 am we are steering out into the Atlantic and keeping towards the coast of Portugal. Evening another religious parody was attempted in our quarters but only about 6 attended. Tyler our steward who had been cursing during the morning took his stand and began to read a dangerously heterodox sermon of which he said the Rev. H.W. Beecher was the author. During the performance he was greeted with groans and cries of "Remember the chees you stole from the passengers yesterday". And a canful of hot coffee was poured from above on him. Bad as he was I felt sorry for him. He abruptly desisted and walked from the stand uttered a horried curse against the sailors. Passed Cape St. Vincent at midnight.'

Monday 1st November. 'Strong head wind impedes progress. At 8 am are opposite Lisbon harbour and at 11.30 opposite the Burlin Islands on our left. The day so much improved in the afternoon that the sea became like a lake and at 8 pm and up to midnight were going along sweetly at 14 miles per hour.'

Tuesday 2nd November. 'About 2 am a great change in the weather took place and at 6 when I went on deck the wind and rain were beating against us and the sea was in a very angry mood indeed. At noon the ship is rolling and pitching until we cannot stand and many are poorly. Lord save us.'

Wednesday 3rd November. 'In the Bay of Biscay again awful weather, a terrible day. God of mercy preserve us for my heart faints as the ponderous seas dash over our bows and make our noble ship tremble as a leaf and stop for the moment as though considering what to do. The angry billows are rising like mountains covered with white foam. Oh the dangers of the deep.'

Thursday 4th November. 'At 4 am passed the Lizard and 8 Eddystone Lighthouse and at 10 arrived and anchored in Plymouth Sound. The sight of old England's shores sent a thrill of joy through the hearts alike of passengers and crew even the good old ship seeming to share in the general rejoicing:
"They may say what they will,
But no Englishman's heart,
What 'ere his condition may be,
But feels a keen pang,
When he's forced to depart,
And a thrill when he comes back to thee.
For whatever thy faults,
Thou art dear to us all,
No matter what strange countries boast,
No blessings are there,
That can ever compare,
With our home on thy sea girded coast.
Then here's to thyself,
Thou wee bonny land,
There's a bumper old England to thee,
Brave sons and fair daughters,
Shall join heart and hand,
And sing Ho for the land of the free."
'At 11.30 weighed anchor and started up the Channel at the entrance of which we passed 81 ships and 14 boats. How spirited we all begin to feel, indeed the thought of home is a tonic both of body and mind.'

Friday 5th November. 'Detained in the Channel by a fog and anchored in the evening about the Downs.'

Saturday 6th November. 'Fog continues and our ship being so large and drawing so much water the pilot is afraid to venture and we are still 10 miles below Gravesend. Wearisome delay but although disappointed at not getting home tonight it is the happiest of the last fifty.'

Sunday 7th November. 'Weighed anchor at 7 am and proceeded up the Thames. Passed hundreds of ships one of which was the "Hooper" which I am told recently landed in one cargo 11,000 tons of grain from America to Liverpool. Arrived in the Royal Albert Dock, London at 5 pm, and proceeded via the Great Northern Railway, home.'

So our travellers are back on dry land again, not having been ashore, as far as we can tell, since leaving Australia on September 21st; at least there is no mention of any member of the family being off the ship. The entire homeward voyage from New Zealand had occupied 56 days or just 30 days less than the 'Westland' under sail alone and without touching land. On the return several stops were made, though none of long duration, and of course the journey was in distance very much shortened by using the Suez Canal.

Thus at that time the difference between steam and sail was not very great if the latter was fortunate with the weather – we read of the 'John Elder' doing 13 miles per hour, which is just over 300 miles per day. Under favourable conditions sailing vessels could easily exceed that figure. As power increased, however, so did speed and a modern vessel could maintain 25/30 miles per hour or three times the speed of the 'John Elder'.

Epilogue

So, somewhat abruptly, we find the Hillary family back home, which can hardly have been what they or their friends expected almost one year previously. This must have been a decided anticlimax, and as they were a day later than they anticipated we imagine there were no scenes comparable to those witnessed on their departure, and in view of the delay probably no reception of any sort. This always reminds me of 'Gondoliers' Act 2, when the Duke arrives in Barataria and feels a little more was to be expected –

'Do I find a guard of honour?'	NO
'The Town illuminated?'	NO
'A Royal salute fired?'	NO
'Triumphal arches erected?'	NO

On the other hand one feels that it must have been with some pleasure they set foot in Tow Law again, and it is to my great regret that I could not have been present at 'My Class' on the following Tuesday. It must have been quite a night and I imagine that on this occasion at least, the Scriptures took a back seat.

I take it that following the various vicissitudes of the Hillarys for almost twelve months must have aroused some interest in what was to become of them, and while I shall endeavour to supply some information, it must be borne in mind that almost 100 years have elapsed and all the actors have left the stage. It has never been clear to me just how my grandfather got back into trade again, but there is no doubt that he became a shopkeeper after their return. It may be that he did not sell up when he left for New Zealand, but left someone in charge. He did leave a brother behind who may have looked after his interests, and who we know later himself emigrated to, of all places, New Zealand. By then, of course, New Zealand had become a much more prosperous place than when John Hillary was there.

The fact that he *was* back in business again is borne out by what my own father – 'Baby Herbert' – once told me of how he got into serious trouble and disgrace. It seems that when in the shop one day the old boy, if I may be so disrespectful, wanted to reach something high up and was foolish enough to place one foot on top of a barrel of treacle. His weight proved too much and the end of the barrel broke leaving Papa with one leg inside and the other outside. Young Herbert, who witnessed the event, could not restrain his mirth and hooted with laughter. It may well have been that as my grandfather was rather on the short side, the accident proved to be more painful than his son realized. But the outcome was that the shop had to be closed while the leg was extracted and the owner changed his trousers. Herbert was later on given a severe lecture, because it was just 'not done' to laugh at a parent in Victorian times, certainly not Papa. An interesting point in passing is that treacle, in those days, came in barrels and was sold loose, and not in tins or jars as is the case today.

I have reason to believe that John Hillary had several shops, because I do know that besides grocery he also dealt in new and secondhand furniture, and household ironmongery. He had a keen eye for business and at that time, I should imagine, was the most successful shopkeeper in Tow Law. My grandmother used to tell me about the first consignment of centre draught lamps he received. To make the matter clear to the modern reader I must explain that previously all of the oil lamps, and most people in Tow Law used no other form of lighting, merely had one, or at most two, flat wicks. The centre draught lamp had a completely

EPILOGUE

circular wick which permitted air to be drawn up the middle giving a very much brighter light, brilliant in fact for those days. John Hillary let it be known to certain of his customers that he was anxious to know how well these new lamps performed, and would they be kind enough to take one home to try, and let him know the result when they brought the lamp back in a few days' time. Grandmother told me how they both went out after dark for a walk along the streets where those customers lived, and how easy it was to see who was using the new lamps. Of course the lamps were never returned, and as expected J.H. was soon selling lamps as fast as he could get delivery.

In the meantime, there is no doubt he continued to be a keen Wesleyan and became, or for all I know, carried on being a local preacher. This necessitated him being away for most Sunday afternoons and evenings and he made many journeys in the surrounding area, a district which could be most inhospitable in the dark winter months. Abiding by the principle that neither one's ox nor ass should be worked on the Sabbath, he steadfastly refused to harness up one of his ponies into a trap, but insisted on doing all these journeys on foot. He did however insist on the usual Sunday roast for dinner, but then oxen and asses don't cook meals.

But to revert, Grandpa would depart, bible in one hand and storm lantern in the other, and knowing the short cuts across the fells would spurn to use the roads. This was quite alright in fine weather but was quite another story when snow began to fall, as anyone who knows the fells will understand. My grandmother was extremely worried on these occasions, and more than once was in the process of organizing a search party when the little preacher emerged from the gloom, to express surprise at all the fuss. I suppose he worked on the assumption that God would look after him, and certainly nothing ever did happen.

Being a non-drinker John Hillary also became involved in the temperance movement, and I have heard him tell about a public meeting which he and his fellow workers organized. It would appear that they arranged for some local big-wig to speak at what they described as a temperance lecture. After the chairman's introduction, no doubt my grandfather, the speaker spoke on the theme of 'Purer Beer for the Working Man'. This was not at all to the liking of the committee members sharing the platform, as they did not believe in beer at all, pure or otherwise. Finally it came to John Hillary's turn to close the meeting and while thanking the speaker mentioned that perhaps they could not all agree with what had been said. Afterwards the speaker was quick to take up this point, and it was explained to him that beer in any form was quite unacceptable. He then pointed out that he believed in temperance, and had not been asked to speak about total abstinence. Strangely, John Hillary had not realised the full significance of these two terms until that time.

At some point there must have come a great change in John Hillary's life because by the time I knew him he was no longer a shopkeeper. This may have come about with the rise of Co-Ops and Multiple Stores. Not perhaps the huge empires which we know today, but certainly by the time I knew Tow Law there had been established some of the large firms well known in the North, and in business to this day. It may well have been that John Hillary saw the red light with the arrival of keen competition, or that one of the multiple firms bought him out. Be that as it may, his life became entirely different, and he seems to have become a sort of Poo Bah with the local council. What his position really was I have been unable to discover, as records of that period no longer exist.

Whatever his position was it entailed a large amount of bookkeeping, and this work he largely did at home in a small room known as the 'office'. He did beautiful writing and figures, and these books were models of neatness. So particular was he that he always bought ink in penny bottles, half of which he always threw away, lest the ink should get thick and cloudy, and at the same time fitted a new nib in his pen – no fountain pens or ball-points in those days. Now it so happened that in the joke-shops of the time one could buy a joke consisting of a penny ink bottle and a large shiny piece of rubber looking exactly like a huge ink blot. The bottle had only to be laid on its side and the illusion was complete. My father purchased one of these and when next we visited Tow Law, choosing a suitable opportunity, by finding one of the account books open and grandfather absent, placed the joke in position, while the rest of us awaited developments. Soon there was the sound of loud lamentations, and we all rushed into the office to see the fun. There was the old gentleman poking the blot with a piece of blotting paper, by

EPILOGUE

which it refused to be absorbed, it was only when the blot began to move across the page leaving a clean sheet behind that truth began to dawn. Thus did Herbert get a little of his own back for the treacle incident, though he had to wait quite a few years.

Whatever John Hillary's interests in the town may have been, he was sufficiently exalted to be in charge of the celebration of King George V's coronation. I can well remember, as a small boy, standing with the crowd at dusk watching my grandfather walk across the field, torch in hand, to light the huge bonfire. Later, with my father and some local worthies, we stood in the dark, looking across the Pennines, noting the other fires that could be seen on the hills for miles around, and identifying them. That was in June 1911, and in three short years we were to be in the throes of the Great War (later known as World War 1) and John Hillary would be dead.

So far the limelight has tended to fall on John Hillary, but we must not forget 'Mamma'. Indeed, she was the one who played the major role in their great adventure, because it is true to say that without her help and co-operation the journey could not have been undertaken. With six children to look after, one a babe in arms, and under the conditions which prevailed on the 'Westland', life cannot have been easy. One is pleased to read, however, that the diarist does mention helping with the baby's washing when mother was indisposed with seasickness. This was most unusual because at that time fathers did not lift a finger to help in the house, that was definitely woman's work. Having paid tribute to Mamma, let us learn a little about her. She lived for some years after the diarist died, and being on her own used to pay us visits, during which time she would tell me about life aboard ship. Unfortunately these were the days before tape recorders, and I never thought of making any notes.

Among other interesting things she used to tell me, were tales of the early days of the railways, because her family, the Bainbridges, were among the early railway pioneers. I think it is safe to say that an uncle of hers was the first railway guard in the world to be killed, and possibly the first public railway employee to lose his life whilst on duty. It would appear that the very early first class carriages were really stage coaches, fitted with iron wheels, and the luggage was carried on the roof. Part of the guard's duty was to attend to this, and while Bainbridge was on the roof checking and securing the luggage he became so engrossed that he forgot the tunnel at Shildon, the parapet of which struck his head and killed him.

It was on account of this interest in railways that my grandmother and grandfather came to meet. When the line was to be constructed through Tow Law, which also happened to be the centre spot, the construction gang chose this town as their headquarters. Miss Bainbridge's father was in charge, and so they took up temporary residence there. In those times it was the practice to work from the centre outwards, the labour being almost entirely by muscle-power, using gangs of navigators, (later to be known as navvies). I understand that Tow Law was like a wild west town, with construction gangs coming in with money in their pockets, and the Irish labourers from the coke ovens over the fells resenting the intrusion of the newcomers. One can well imagine what happened when the drink began to flow. My great-grandfather was the colliery manager and something of a power in the land, while Bainbridge himself was a person of some importance, so it was inevitable that the families should meet. Thus John Hillary met and married Elizabeth Bainbridge.

Railway enthusiasts might be interested to learn that it was members of the Bainbridge family who were responsible for the construction of the line from Darlington to York, still considered one of the best sections of track engineering in the country. In this case it was Uncle and nephew, the latter surveying and Uncle in charge of the actual construction.

From this point on our two main characters lived their lives together and much that has already been written covers the activities of my grandmother also. There is no doubt that she took an active interest in John Hillary's affairs, and was of considerable help to him in the running of the shops. Probably, in her own quiet way, she was in fact the power behind the throne. I used to gain the impression that Mamma did not always share her husband's religious enthusiasm, though paying lip service. Despite the lack of fire and brimstone I do know that she did many good deeds and gave help when it was needed. Having never had any illness or suffered even a headache, she had scant sympathy for any such sufferer. We do know that she was seasick, and of course, she had seven children, a further daughter Ethel, being born after their return. That apart, she never knew what illness meant, until the one and only occasion from which she never recovered.

It was not that she did not take any risks, because she used to tell me of the time when Tow Law was stricken with the dreaded smallpox, a plague which was a killer – chance of recovery being no higher than 50/50 or possibly even less – and people were dying in their scores. She, realizing that the local doctor, Dr. Hood, was almost 'out on his feet' with lack of sleep and overwork, volunteered to help and became his unpaid nurse and assistant. She spent weeks on this work, and neither she nor the doctor were in any way affected. One day, while on her rounds, she once told me she had heard the sound of singing coming from one of the houses, and knowing that the sole occupant an old lady was dying, she went upstairs to investigate. There she found the doctor sitting on the bed with his arms round the old dear, with tears streaming down his cheeks giving his rendition of 'Safe in the arms of Jesus'. It appears that the old soul, knowing she was dying, requested that the doctor should sing a hymn, and he knowing that he could now do nothing more obliged with probably the only hymn he knew. Even the National Health Service does not cater for such a situation.

Thus began a friendship which lasted for many years, and as the family were now off hand, and Dr. Hood being unmarried, he came to live with the Hillarys, and ran his surgery from their house. He was a Scot, and always called my grandmother 'Luz'. She helped him with his bills which were never sent to the poor, but the amounts were doubled in the case of those who could pay, but unfortunately did not always do so. When the old doctor died the whole town turned out to see the cortege pass.

John Hillary died in 1914 just before the Great War, and so was spared its horrors, but the old lady lived on for some years. She was a prodigious knitter, and while the war lasted knitted socks for soldiers. She set herself the target of a pair per day or seven pairs per week. This amounts to 14 separate socks per week, which any person having a knowledge of knitting knows is quite an output, and in the course of four years she must have produced many hundreds of pairs. In order, I feel, to avoid the rigours of winter at Tow Law, in later years she developed the habit of spending much of the year visiting her many relatives and friends, and thus spent long periods at my home. She seemed to get along very well with my mother and they made garments for distribution mostly among the many grandchildren. I would hear the old treadle sewing machine in use to midnight and after. It was from our house that she set off for home in 1923, calling on her sister in Shildon en route. She never reached Tow Law alive, as she was taken ill for the first and last time.

The main characters having now departed it only remains for us to learn what happened to the other six. This number had, of course, been increased to seven, by the birth of a daughter, Ethel, but as she did not take part in the journey I will, to avoid confusion, leave her out of the picture. There is, however, one point of interest with Ethel, in that she became an aunt of mine twice over. The reason for this being that while my mother married Herbert, my mother's brother, George, married Ethel, thus brother and sister married brother and sister. So, returning to the six in whom we have a special interest, by the time I was born, the son of 'Baby Herbert', my Aunt and Uncles were all grown up with families of their own. Thus I have no knowledge of their early years, other than mentioned in the diary and what I have gleaned from family gossip. We do know that the two older boys, 'Willie' and 'John Tom', were in their teens, as they were accommodated in the single men's quarters on the 'Westland', leaving only Albert, Edith, Fred, and Baby Herbert with their parents.

Before dealing with the future of these people, I must digress and explain something which was greatly to influence their lives, particularly those of Willie and John. Although John Hillary was such an ardent Methodist, strange to relate, his children did not follow in his footsteps, with perhaps the exception of Albert. The rest of the children became attracted to the Salvation Army, and two of the sons, as I shall later explain made this a source of livelihood. The reason for this attraction was most likely two-fold; in the first place all the children were very musical and they found the services at the Salvation Army more to their liking than the mere hymn-singing of the Wesleyans. The Salvation Army had its many bands and there was much music and singing. Less Hell-fire was preached and though it may have been believed in was rather swept under the

EPILOGUE

carpet. Thus their services tended to be much livelier and jollier than the churches and chapels provided. Secondly, just as is the case today, the younger members began to view religion in a different light, but felt they must attend some form of service, this being almost instinctive; so they turned to what today might be termed a break-away group. The Salvation Army filled this need, and with the exception mentioned all the brothers met their respective partners because of this interest. My father and Uncle Fred did, in fact, become Band Masters when they moved to Scotland, at Partick and Govan, and it was at Partick that I first saw the light of day. In later life they all, except Willie and John, left the Army and returned, as it were, to the fold. Fred was for many years choir master at Ilford, and my father Sunday School Superintendant at Whitefield, near Manchester.

Let us now pass on to the eldest child, Willie. He was the humourist of the family, with a ready wit and in my opinion should have made a career on the stage, but as we have heard became deeply involved in the Salvation Army. It was most likely because of his religious background he never gave the theatre any consideration, but he was a born showman, and his life with the Army took him into the limelight which he undoubtedly loved. I think I can safely say, from personal knowledge, that it was not really the religious angle that appealed to him but his natural ability to attract people. The plain truth is, he was one of the original 'Penny-on-the-Drum' men, and with his wife toured all over the country in that capacity. Perhaps I should explain to the modern reader that revivalist meetings were not only a means of enlisting new recruits but a great source of revenue. Willie was an accomplished player on a Wheatstone concertina which in his skilled hands was a wonderful instrument; he was a very fine singer and his wife also. They would attend these meetings singing solos and duets, and after each item there was always a request for more pennies to be thrown on the drum. Such an item as 'The Bible my Mother gave to me' would produce a veritable shower.

His ability to attract people had the same effect on animals. Snappy dogs would be as clay in his hands, and he really could charm the birds from the trees. He would give a whistle and they would fly down when he could feed them like the pigeons in Trafalgar Square. This all led him to a great interest in household pets, mostly cats and dogs, and he acquired some skill as an amateur vet providing of course no surgery was entailed. He used to tell how some of his lady clients would bring their overfed poodles to him because they were off their food. After 'treatment' he would meet the owner to be told that 'Fido is all right now, and quite ravenous', and he used to say 'so would she be if she hadn't eaten for a week'. But he was quite skilful in cases of real sickness and often made no charge for his services. His own special love was for Yorkshire terriers, of which he became a fairly successful breeder. Of his passing I know neither the time nor the place, but that he is with us no more is quite certain. I only remember him as a very jolly person and good company.

While on the subject of the Salvationists we must turn to 'John Tom', who was the next eldest and who also made a career in this movement. He rose to the exalted rank of Colonel and was always known as 'the Colonel' to the family. He had the largest family, mostly girls; there seemed so many that when visiting I was never quite sure who were friends and who were relations. There was only one son, Luther, whose working life was spent at Barclays and doubtless many will remember him there. The Colonel also married a Salvationist who in turn rose to high rank, equal with that of her husband I believe. These two also toured the country preaching at the various Army Citadels for which they gained a great reputation. There is no doubt all the Hillary brothers were fine public speakers, and Uncle John was no exception. Later the family moved to Kingston, Jamaica, where the Colonel was in charge of all the Salvation Army activities in the West Indies. Unfortunately, in the end the heat proved too trying for my Uncle, who by then was no longer a young man, and with great regret the family had to return. His subsequent illness forced an early retirement but after making a full recovery, he remained very active until the end. During this period he had many irons in the fire, being of too active a disposition to sit about at home, and for some time was responsible for the religious texts which many readers may have seen in the London Underground trains.

Next in line of succession we come to Albert, the most successful of the brothers, commerically speaking. Of his very early life I have no knowledge, and by the time I knew him he

EPILOGUE

was co-director of Carson's Chocolates. Apart from producing very high class confectionery, the firm was fortunate in discovering a line which turned out to be a real money spinner. This was Carson's Milk Chocolate Cubes, which many older readers may remember. This caused great expansion of the factory and was doubtless the reason for them selling out to another chocolate firm, and brings us up to that event which ran through all our lives, the Great War. After this Uncle Albert bought a firm which had previously imported continental chocolate and confectionery machinery, where his previous knowledge of the

trade proved most useful. In this business, for a time, my father joined him, as we shall see later. The Hillary family were always staunch Liberals and Albert was selected to be candidate for the Harwich division, which he contested successfully. Thus for a time he represented that division in the House, and it is interesting to remember that this was the same division which the famous diarist Pepys also represented. Uncle Albert lived for some years at Ardleigh in Essex, and finally retired to Frinton, where he died.

Next we turn to the only girl of the party, Edith. My earliest recollection of her is being Mrs. Taylor, having married a Welshman of that name, who thus became my Uncle Sam. They lived for many years at Porth in the Rhondda, where Sam Taylor was a very successful wholesale sweet merchant. Unfortunately, in later years my Aunt Edith was afflicted with a serious illness which ended with her losing the use of her legs, and she was bedridden for several years before she died.

Fred is the next on our list, and it so happens that he, of all my Uncles, was the one I knew best. My own family moved from the North to Ilford in Essex and living there at that time was my Uncle and his family. By now he was London Sales Manager for Carsons, the firm that brother Albert had previously been connected with. Thus my Uncle Fred, his son, my cousin Horace, and I spent a great deal of time together. In photography, cycling, and radio, then known as wireless, we had a common interest which passed many happy hours. In those days the film camera was not used by the more serious photographer, and so we sallied forth with plate camera, a set of loaded plate slides and a folding wooden tripod, all of which was fairly bulky and heavy. Thus equipped we would wander through the local parks and countryside (there was plenty of country round Ilford at that time), in search of suitable subjects. On returning we would lose ourselves in the cellar which having no window made an excellent darkroom, and there with the aid of a red lamp and suitable trays we would proceed to develop the results of our labours. It was then that I learned that Uncle Fred was no amateur, and had been at one time in business at Tow Law as the sole professional photographer. From him I learned many useful tips, little of which would be of any use today.

About this time wireless telephony was in its infancy, and Uncle Fred and I obtained what were then known as Experimenter's Licences. There were no regular broadcasts, and of course no B.B.C., and most of us constructed sets from parts purchased from the wireless shops, and of course we all had outside aerials, on high poles erected in the garden. I well remember an occasion, when we were expecting a very special programme in the evening, and knowing there was an experimental transmission in the morning, my Uncle decided to check that his set was working. It was just as well because there wasn't a sound from it. The valves glowed brightly, everything seemed in order, but nothing emerged. We then proceeded to take everything to pieces, and spent a long time on this, but in the end we were left with what looked like several cigar boxes with light bulbs on top, and still nothing. It was at this point that my Aunt came in and informed my Uncle that she had removed the aerial lead-in wire, because her washing was blowing up against it. At this point I decided it was time for me to have an urgent appointment elsewhere, and made a hurried departure.

We spent many hours cycling, most cycles then being of the

EPILOGUE

'sit up and beg' type, and in warmer weather we wore straw boaters for headgear. Looking back, I can think of no more uncomfortable and useless form of head covering. Strangely enough no man appeared outside without his head being covered, and the 'no hat brigade' were looked upon as a crowd of cranks. About the mid-twenties Uncle Fred moved to Bristol to become Sales Manager for the firm at their headquarters, but soon became very ill and died there.

We are now down to 'Baby Herbert', my father, about whom I should know the most, but of his earlier years I have only vicarious knowledge. I do know that he was educated at Wolsingham Grammar School, after which he served an apprenticeship in painting and decorating, and thus earned his Master Painter's certificate. Perhaps I should point out here that it was customary for a young man to first learn a trade, the reason for this being that should he later fall on hard times he always had something he could turn to. Of course, it was inevitable I should hear about this seven years as an apprentice, and what working conditions were like. There were no ready-made paints, and a man had to mix his own for each job, and know what colours to use. They had to push their trestles and ladders etc., on a hand-cart, and as the job might be several miles away, in a very hilly district this could be quite hard work. Wages were paid from the time of arrival at the job, time taken to get there and back did not count, and at the end of the day you mixed your paints etc. ready for the next morning.

After his initial training my father did start up in business on his own, but was forced to close down, about which he was very bitter. The reason for this was that many of the colliers when not at work, would do other people's decorating quite cheaply when it required no special tackle. My father was thus left only the staircases and more difficult jobs requiring equipment, while the more lucrative work was done by others. Now the trade unions had been formed he felt, rightly or wrongly, each man should stick to his own trade, and not encroach on the living of others. He closed the business down and removed to Partick, where he ran an office in Glasgow for a wallpaper firm, and it was at this point that I came on the scene.

It was of course to be some years before I was able to take an active interest in my family's affairs. By this time we had moved to Whitefield near Manchester, via I am told, Carlisle, but of all this I have no knowledge. Herbert had now found himself a job as a commercial traveller, in these days called a rep, with the firm of Baxendales. He was to stay with them for many years, calling on decorators where his specialised knowledge stood him in good stead. Having a large area to cover, mostly on the eastern side of the country, from Suffolk to the Scottish border, he was away all week and was only home at weekends. We lived in Lancashire all through the Great War, and my father had to do work of national importance as a labourer at British Dyes at Huddersfield. He had almost no sight in the right eye, and was thus no use for active service. I well remember the signing of the Armistice on 11th November 1918, my father was back home by midday, not even having bothered to collect any wages due to him, and by the next week he was back on the road at his old job.

The reader will doubtless remember that by now brother Albert was engaged in the chocolate and confectionery machinery trade, and he asked my father to come to London and join him. So we moved again, settling for some years at Ilford. Later my father decided he could do better on his own account, and as I was now in my early twenties, we joined forces. Unfortunately, after some years and with the approach of another war causing an arms race on the Continent, we as importers faced difficulties in carrying on and had to close down. It was not only a difficult time, but a sad one also, because of my mother's sudden death from cancer. In due course my father married again, and from then on until his death from congestion of the lungs, lived in semi-retirement in Birmingham.

That should have been the end of the Hillary saga, and it's associations with Tow Law, but for the fact that my unmarried sister, Maude, finding herself alone, decided to go back and live there. She now lives in a splendid, modern, old peoples' home, where she has a self-contained flat with all mod. cons. Thus we are back to Tow Law again, and should any of my readers find themselves driving up the old Drovers Road which runs right through the town, perhaps they might spare a thought for the Hillarys and their abortive journey to New Zealand.

Appendix

Iron-hulled ship-rigged vessel 'WESTLAND'
Built by Robert Duncan & Co., Port Glasgow, and completed in October, 1878.
1,186 tons gross
1,116 tons net
1,0458 tons under deck
Length – 222.8 ft.
Breadth – 35.1 ft.
Depth – 22.5 ft.
Length of poop – 35 ft.
Length of forecastle – 36 ft.
Official Number – 80423
Signal Letters – W.V.P.C.
Port of Registry – Glasgow
Classed 100 A1 by Lloyd's Register

Voyage of 1879–1880
Sailed London 21st November, 1879
Passed Deal 22nd November, in tow of tug 'BEN NEVIS'
Arrived Plymouth 24th November
Sailed Plymouth 27th November
Spoken in position lat. 42 N., long. 17 W., 29th November
Arrived Lyttelton 21st February, 1880.

Iron screw barque 'JOHN ELDER'
Built by J. Elder & Co., Glasgow, and completed in August, 1870.
Owners – Pacific Steam Navigation Co., of Liverpool
4,160 tons gross.
2,431 tons net.
3,215 tons builders' measurement.
Length – 406.4 ft.
Breadth – 41.5 ft.
Depth – 35.2 ft.
Machinery – Compound steam engine developing 550 nominal horsepower, manufactured by J. Elder & Co.
Official Number – 63313.
Signal Letters – V.Q.L.M.
Accommodation for 1,015 passengers.

APPENDIX

On 18th January, 1892, when on a voyage from Valparaiso to Liverpool with copper bars, ingots and ore, silver ore, and general cargo, the 'JOHN ELDER' ran ashore at Carranza Point, about 65 miles north of Talcahuano, and became a total loss. Her crew and passengers were saved.

Voyage of 1880
  Sailed Adelaide 23rd September, 1880
  At Suez 21st October
  Arrived Naples 26th October
  Sailed Naples 27th October
  Arrived off Plymouth 3rd November
  Sailed from off Plymouth 4th November
  Arrived London 7th November

Iron-hulled steamer 'TARARUA'
  Built by Gourlay Bros., Dundee, in 1864.
  Owners – Union Steamship Co. Ltd., of Welllington.
  830 tons gross.
  692 tons net.
  523 tons under deck.
  Length – 222.6 ft.
  Breadth – 28 ft.
  Depth – 16.2 ft.
  Machinery – Compound steam engine developing 155 nominal horsepower, manufactured by Gourlay Bros.
  Official Number – 50088.
  Signal Letters – W.M.L.V.
  Wrecked off Waipapa Point, New Zealand, on 28th April, 1881.